Amelia Earhart

Mercy Otis Warren

- *A Doll Maker's Workbook* -

SIX FAMOUS AMERICAN WOMEN

by Lauren Welker

Mary Cassatt

Margaret Sanger

Published By   HOBBY HOUSE PRESS, INC.
Cumberland, Maryland 21502

Dedication

This book is dedicated to the memory of Sophia Welker.

Additional Copies of this Book may be Purchased at $5.95
from
HOBBY HOUSE PRESS, INC.
900 Frederick Street
Cumberland, Maryland 21502
or from your favorite bookstore or dealer.
Please add $1.25 per copy postage.

© 1986 by Lauren Welker
All rights reserved. No part of this book may be reproduced or utilized in any form or by any means electronic or mechanical, including photocopying, records, or by any information storage and retrieval system, without permission in writing from the publisher. Inquiries should be addressed to Hobby House Press, Inc., 900 Frederick Street, Cumberland, Maryland 21502.
Printed in the United States of America.
ISBN: 0-87588-290-0

Table of Contents

Introduction 4
Planning Your Doll 5
Sculpting 5
Baking 6
Painting 6
Body Patterns 7
Felt Body 8
Some Useful Sewing Techniques 10
Grandma Moses 11
Amelia Earhart 14
Mary Cassatt 17
Mercy Otis Warren 20
Margaret Sanger 24
Harriet Tubman 27
Where To Buy Supplies 30
Large Size Patterns 31
Bibliography 47

Grandma Moses

Harriet Tubman

Introduction

This book is designed to teach the basics of making a quality original doll. How good your dolls will be depends on you. I have found that persistence is more important than talent. Be willing to discard what does not work and start over.

On the other hand, do not be so critical of yourself that you never finish a project. Finishing a doll is the first step on the path to good doll making. Each one you make will be a little better and you will learn something new each time. Do not be afraid to experiment. You may discover a better way to do things.

No matter how busy you are, you can find time to do the things you really want to do. Take a tray with your clay and tools to the T.V. room in the evening. Work on hands and feet. They do not require much concentration. By the time you get to the head, the momentum will carry you through.

Take good care of your supplies and tools. Keep them together so you do not have to hunt for something every time you want to work on your dolls. Disorganization discourages effort.

Do not cut out your patterns. Take the time to trace them, adjusting each one for your doll. Everyone works a little differently. If you want to use a pattern later and have lost a piece, you can trace another.

Buy a box of envelopes and use it for a pattern file. Label each envelope with the name of the pattern and file them alphabetically.

Enjoy what you are doing. Do not compare your work to that of other people. If theirs is better, you may become discouraged and quit. If it is worse, you may become overconfident and cease to improve. The only true competition exists within yourself to do the best work that you can do and that is competition enough since few of us ever realize that goal.

Look at other people's work with the object of learning from them. What makes a certain doll so appealing? How are those eyes painted?

Share information with others. There is little danger of my making your doll or your making mine. We are all individuals.

Planning Your Doll

The patterns in this book are in the scale of one inch to the foot (3 to 31cm). The average doll will be 5½in (14cm) tall and suitable for use with furniture and accessories scaled one inch to the foot (3 to 31cm). These patterns may also be used to assemble porcelain doll kits in the same scale.

Not everyone adapts to this tiny scale right off so in the back of the book the patterns are reproduced in a 50 percent larger size for those who wish to make a larger doll.

Two body patterns are given, one for use with full length arms and legs and one for use with half arms and legs.

Some people prefer making wrapped bodies. If you would like to try this, a diagram is included. First, the finished body parts are glued onto a wire skeleton called an armature. Then the body is wrapped using strips of gauze or nylon stocking. Cotton balls may be used for padding where needed. Know what you want your doll to do and you will choose the right body.

Sculpting

The head, arms and legs are modeled from a polyform clay which can be baked in your home oven and is available from craft shops. Common brand names are Fimo, Sculpey and Sculpey II. This clay will not shrink when baking. The packaging states that after it has been baked, it can be carved and sanded; however, I recommend that you do not bake a piece until you are satisfied with it because sanding or carving may uncover imperfections in the clay that would render a piece unacceptable. I especially like the way flesh colored Fimo looks when it has been baked and finished with a matte varnish, but you can substitute any clay that does not shrink as it hardens.

My favorite tools for modeling small scale dolls are an old fashioned orange stick (used for manicures, it has a point at one end and a rounded edge at the other end), small metal manicure tools and toothpicks. You can use an emery board to sand a toothpick or small dowel rod into a usable shape for sculpting. Sculpey makes a set of tools for use with its product that is nice but a little large for our purposes. Art stores may carry some small tools that you would find useful.

The clay is stiff when removed from the box or package. The heat from your body will soften it and make it more workable. You might hold a little in your hands to warm it up. Another method is to put a little in a plastic bag and sit on it for awhile. Think of it as passive preparation.

To model the shoulder head begin with a little ball of tin foil for the head and cover it with clay. This will keep the head from getting too heavy. The foil does not have to be removed either before or after baking. First, model the general shape of the shoulder head using the diagram for size and not worrying about the facial details. STAY IN SCALE! You might use a second piece of foil for the opening at the shoulders to hold the shape. This piece will be removed after the baking. Add clay for the nose, chin and forehead. If your first efforts at modeling eyes and lips are not satisfactory, you might consider painting them on. It is more important to complete your first project than it is to be perfect. Skill comes with practice.

To model the hands, start with a mitten shape. Make sure the hands are to scale before refining them. I use my toothpick to divide the large part of the mitten into four fingers. If I wish to separate the fingers, I use a sharp craft knife. If the hands get too soft and floppy as you work on them, set them aside awhile. As they cool down, the clay will become a bit firmer. Before baking, use your toothpick to make a hole in each arm for a wire.

Form the feet, keeping in mind the style shoes you will be painting on them. Make the general shape and heel height. Details can be painted on. Do not forget to make a hole for the wire in each leg before baking.

There is a tendency for clay parts to "grow" as you work on them. When you have a few pieces that you are satisfied with, bake them. Check the scale constantly. Try not to have two left feet. Look at your own hands and feet if you are not sure how they should look.

See Illustration 1 on page 6.

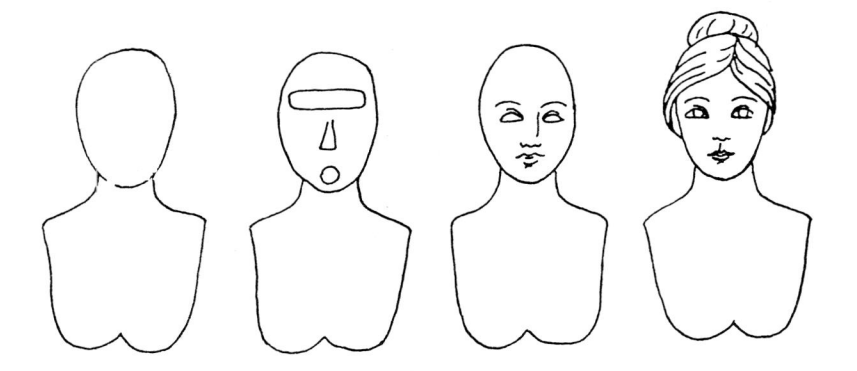

Illustration 1.
First make the basic shoulder head shape using the diagram on page 7 to check the scale. Next add extra clay for the nose, chin and forehead. Refine the features addition clay where need. Last, do not forget the ears. If you prefer modeled and painted hair to a wig, add that now.

Baking

Follow the instructions on your clay. Is your oven fast (food cooks in less than the allotted time)? Is your oven slow (cooking takes longer)? Make allowances for this with your clay. I prefer to bake mine in a white baking dish rather than a cookie sheet. Do not despair if you overcook your clay and it turns brown. You can paint over it with flesh tone paint.

Do not forget — if you are using a wire armature body, you must make the holes for the wire before baking the pieces. Use your toothpick and poke a hole in the top of each limb (and through the neck of the shoulder head for a wrapped body). The holes should be large enough to accommodate a light wire (available at the hardware store), a pipe cleaner, or chenille strip.

Painting

The dolls in this book were painted using Duncan Bisq-stain and brushes in sizes 3, 6/0 and 10/0 purchased at a ceramic shop. You can use any good quality liquid acrylic paint. Basic colors to have on hand are white, blue, brown, black, red and a flesh tone if needed.

The doll may be painted before or after assembling, whichever you find easier. Start with the whites of the eyes on dolls made from flesh colored clay. See diagram. Be sure the eyes are evenly spaced from the nose. Next, paint in the iris, the colored part of the eye. Add a thin line of black under the upper lid and add a black pupil. Eyelashes may be added if desired but they are tricky to paint. In real life we seldom notice the eyelashes as a separate entity.

Next add the eyebrows. Use a medium brown paint for blondes and red heads, dark brown for brunettes, and black for raven-haired ladies.

Continued on page 8.

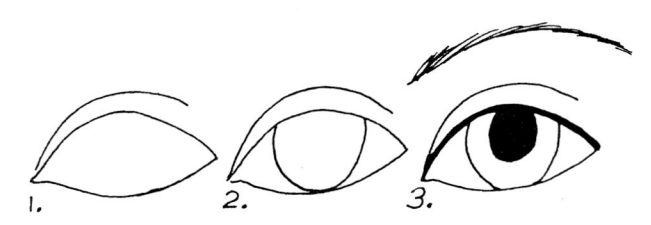

Illustration 2.
1. Paint the whites of the eyes.
2. Paint the iris. You may also paint the upper lid a subtle shadow tone if desired.
3. Paint a black line under the upper lid. Paint the pupil. Add a softly arched eyebrow.

Body Patterns

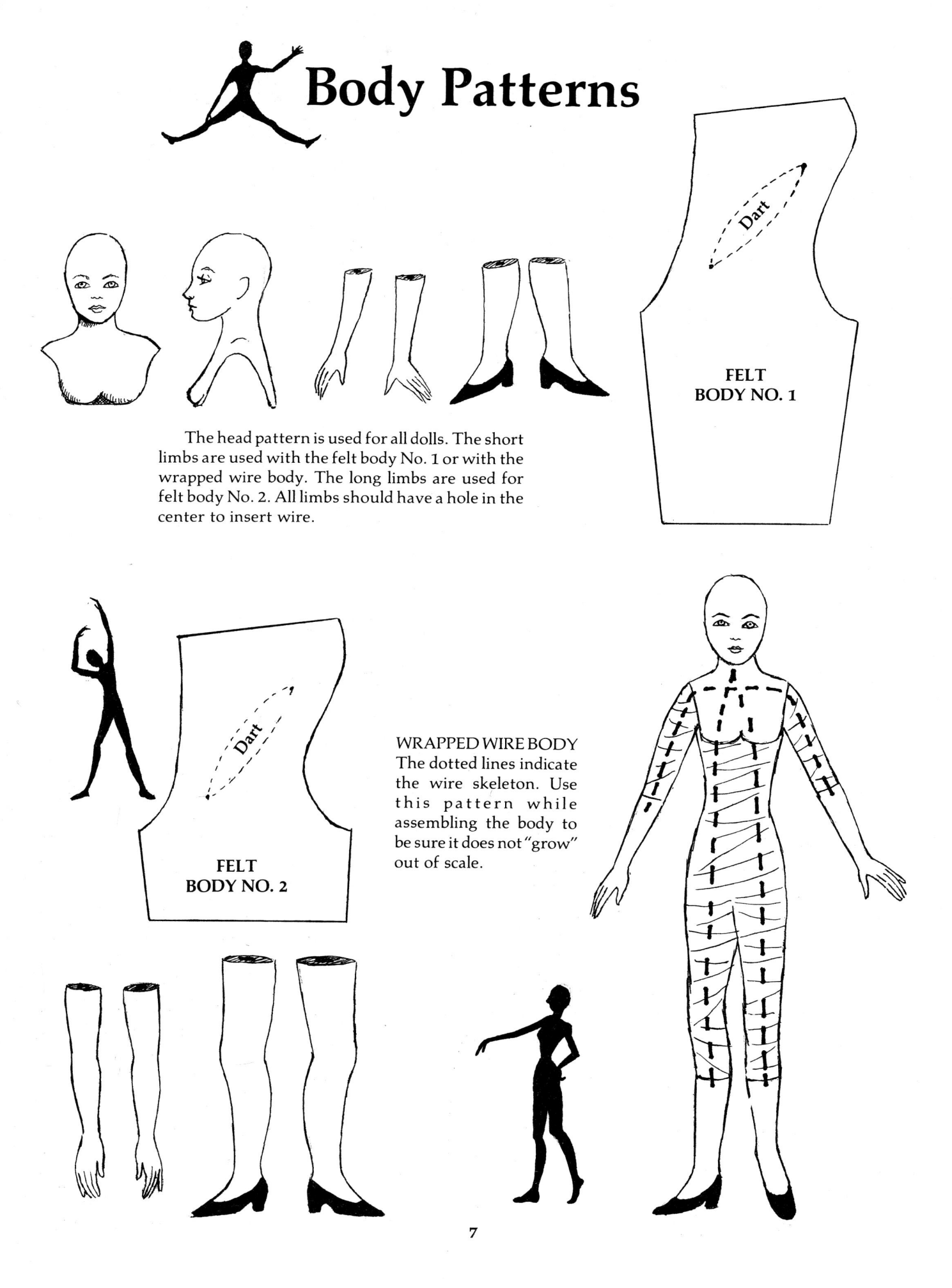

The head pattern is used for all dolls. The short limbs are used with the felt body No. 1 or with the wrapped wire body. The long limbs are used for felt body No. 2. All limbs should have a hole in the center to insert wire.

FELT BODY NO. 1

FELT BODY NO. 2

WRAPPED WIRE BODY
The dotted lines indicate the wire skeleton. Use this pattern while assembling the body to be sure it does not "grow" out of scale.

Mix a little flesh tone with your lip color and paint the lips. Using the color full strength and your smallest brush, add a thin line between the lips. A faint outline as it appears on some of the finer antique bisque dolls can also be effective if subtly done.

Paint the doll's shoes, keeping in mind the fashion era that your doll will represent. Brown soles and black pumps go with most styles.

Use a clear matte spray sealer or an acrylic matte varnish to give your parts a nice finish and protect your paint.

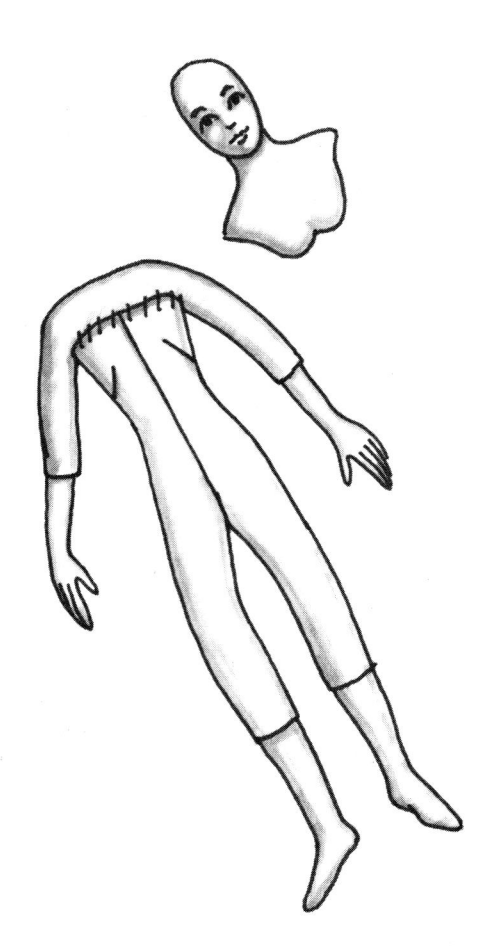

Felt Body

Cut two body pieces for each body. Sew darts, if any. Sew center front seam. Sew center back seam. Matching the center front and center back seams at the crotch, sew the leg seam. Your body should remind you of a pair of tall slacks. Turn right side out using a hemostat, surgical clamp, or tweezers.

If you find that turning the body is too great an aggravation, hand sew your bodies and do not turn them. Eliminate any unreasonable frustration. This is supposed to be fun.

Fit a leg in each opening. If the hole is too tight, stretch it gently with a pencil or the round handle of your seam ripper. Glue a pipe cleaner (chenille strip or wire) in each clay leg. Let dry. Run a row of glue around the inside of each body leg. White glue or tacky glue is fine for this job. Insert a leg in each opening. Be sure that the toes are facing forward. Let dry.

Give the pipe cleaner a few twists and cut off the excess at the top of the body with a wire clipper. Borrow this from your husband if necessary but if you continue doll making, you will want to invest in one of your own. Stuff your body using the hemostat or tweezers. Sew the top closed.

Glue the arms onto a piece of pipe cleaner (chenille strip or wire) that you have trimmed to the proper length. The arms should measure about 5in (13cm) from finger tip to finger tip. Cover with a tube of felt glued over the wire armature.

Sew the arm tube onto the body, being sure that the arms will be the right length and even on each side of the body.

Glue the head in place. Let dry.

1. Model and fire clay parts. Sew felt body.
2. Glue wire or pipe cleaner in both legs and one arm.
3. Glue legs into felt body.
4. Stuff body and sew the top closed. Measure the arms, trim the wire and glue the second arm in place.
5. Cover the arm tube with felt. Glue in place.
6. Sew the arm tube to the body. Glue the head in place.

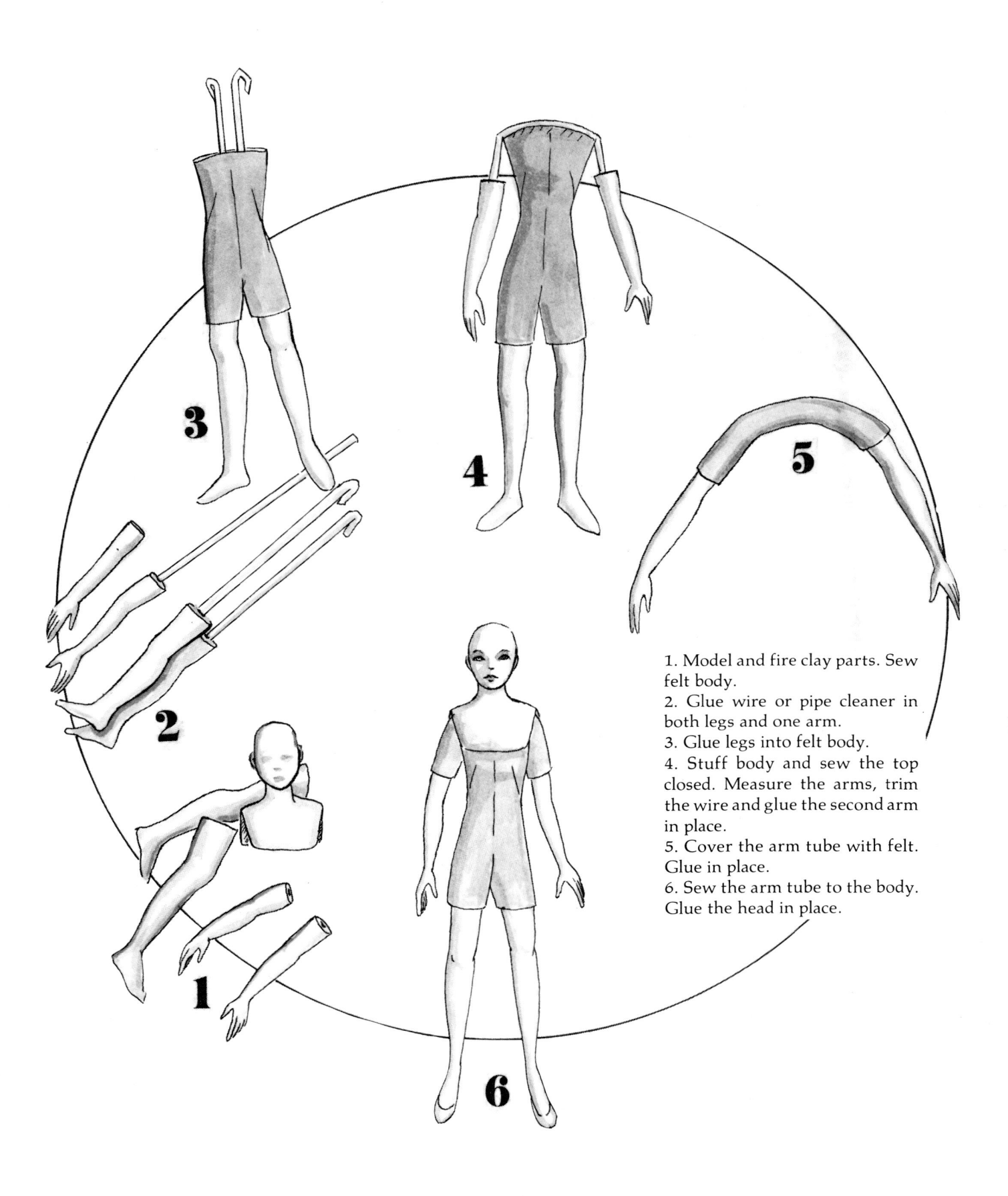

Some Useful Sewing Techniques

Most sewing techniques on a small scale focus on eliminating bulk and creating a natural effect. The clothing is actually built onto the doll using a combination of sewing and gluing. A glue applicator that is shaped like a plastic syringe is useful for making thin lines of glue. It can be loaded with any good quality white glue. Too much glue will show through the fabric so neatness counts. An alternate way of applying glue is to make a puddle of glue on a dish and apply it in small amounts with a toothpick.

Necklines can be tricky. A real facing would be too bulky for a neat finish. On a simple untrimmed neckline I make a facing from lightweight iron-on innerfacing. First cut a square of innerfacing larger than needed. Pin it to the bodice, right sides together. (The sticky side of the innerfacing faces away from the garment.) Carefully, by hand or by machine, sew around the neckline, making an even circle. Cut your innerfacing away so it looks like a real facing. Turn and press in place.

The high collar is a popular feature on many turn-of-the-century styles. It is a very simple finish. Run a light touch of glue around the neck opening and let dry to prevent raveling. Hand sew 1/8in (0.3cm) ribbon along the right side of the neck opening to form the collar. Silk ribbon works best.

If you do not have ribbon to coordinate with your outfit, you may make an 1/8in (0.3cm) strip by applying some iron-on innerfacing along the selvage on the wrong side of your material. Cut to size. Apply as you would the ribbon.

Chainette (also called Bunka) is often used as a finish or trim. It is first unraveled. A line of glue is applied where the trim will go. Then the Chainette is pressed in place by hand.

Trims on bodices and skirts are often glued in place on little garments. Rows of lace, ribbon, Chainette or fringe are commonly used. Bows and "buttons" (usually tiny beads) are also glued on.

Hems may be handled in several ways. They may be turned up and sewn or glued, or they may be faced with tulle if they threaten to unravel.

Felt has many uses as it is not subject to unraveling. Try it for hats, collars, cuffs, and belts.

Always work "on the flat" as much as possible, applying neck treatments, sleeves and trims before sewing the side seams.

A large skirt or a ruffle can be neatly gathered with a minimum of bulk by overcasting the edge by hand, then gently pulling the threads to gather. This takes a little practice as too small stitches will not gather and too large ones will make bulky gathers.

OVERCASTING

Grandma Moses *was made with short legs and arms (see body instructions) so she could be posed in this chair. Chair and corsage made by Genevieve Emerick.*

GRANDMA MOSES

Born Anna Mary Robertson on September 7, 1860, she left home at the tender age of 12 to earn a living as a hired girl. She later wrote, "This was a grand education for me, in cooking, housekeeping, in moralizing and mingling with the outside world."

In the Autumn of 1887 she married Thomas Moses, a farmer. They moved to Virginia to farm and had ten children. Five of those children died before they moved on to New York State in 1907.

In January of 1927 her husband died. Her youngest son and his wife took over running the farm and Grandma Moses took up painting and making yarn pictures. She was 67 years old.

Her paintings were first displayed in Hoosick Falls, New York, where they were spotted by art collector Louis Caldor in 1938. In 1939, he entered three of her paintings in a show of "Contemporary Unknown Painters" at the Museum of Modern Art in New York City.

She had her first one woman show in October of 1940. She was 80 years old. She enjoyed great success and was quite surprised at the prices her paintings commanded. Grandma Moses, hired girl, farm wife and internationally known artist continued working right up until her death in December of 1961. She was a very young 101 years old.

THE FACE: In modeling Grandma Moses' head, remember that in thinner older folks the ears and nose become more prominent. Gravity has worked over the years to make everything a bit droopy. The tendons in the neck become prominent. The mouth area sinks a bit and lines appear around the mouth and eyes.

THE HAIR: This wig is made from a mohair curl that has been carefully combed through with a large needle. Pieces of the curl are glued neatly around the hairline. When the glue is dry, the rest is twisted into a bun on top and glued in place.

CUTTING: From white cotton cut two underpants and one slip. From black (I used velvet, but cotton would be easier for a beginner) cut one bodice, two sleeves, and one skirt. From pink felt cut two body pieces.

HAVE ON HAND: 3/8in (1cm) white lace for the cuffs, a large lace motif, perhaps cut from a larger piece of lace, for the collar (a floral design that fits the space, for instance), and 1/8in (0.3cm) black grosgrain ribbon for the belt. Extra lace can be used on the undies.

BODY: See general instructions.

UNDERPANTS: Glue lace to the bottom edge of each leg so that it covers the raw edge. Sew the center front seam. Sew the center back seam up to the dot. Sew the leg seam, matching front to back at the crotch. Turn and put on doll. Sew up the center back by hand and gather the waist if needed.

SLIP: Glue lace along the bottom of the slip covering the raw edge. Sew up the center back seam to the dot. Put on doll. Sew up the rest of the center back by hand. Gather the waist in place and knot tightly. Put a dot of glue on your knot.

BODICE: Glue the lace motif in place on the right side of the bodice so that it will form a collar. Trim around the neck. Glue securely at the neckline. Run a line of glue along the bottom edge of each sleeve so it does not ravel. Let dry. Gather the top edge of each sleeve and set into the armholes, sewing by hand if necessary. The gathers should all be adjusted to the center of the sleeve. Sew the underarm/side seams. Turn and place on doll. Sew up the center back by hand. Tuck a little stuffing under the bodice front to make the droopy bosomed look of an older woman. Run a row of gathering stitches around the waist. To make the ruffled cuffs, cut two pieces of 3/8in (1cm) lace 3¾in (10cm) long. Glue into circles. Gather the tops with an overcast stitch and glue in place on each sleeve. Glue unraveled Chainette around the neckline. The "pin" on my doll is a small plastic jewelry finding glued in place. The corsage is fashioned from silk ribbon and is not necessary if you do not desire one.

SKIRT: Turn up a hem and sew by hand. Sew up the center back to the dot. Place on doll. Finish sewing up the center back. Gather at the waist and knot securely. Cover the waist with a belt made from the 1/8in (.3cm) black grosgrain ribbon. A small buckle can be fashioned from wire if you wish.

GLASSES: Using the thinnest wire that you can find, twist two lengths together to form the first temple. Use a paint brush handle to form the lens area. Twist a bit to form the bridge and use the paint brush again to form the next "lens." Continue twisting to form the final temple. Cut and bend the temples to the correct shape. I cannot give you exact measurements because the glasses should fit your doll.

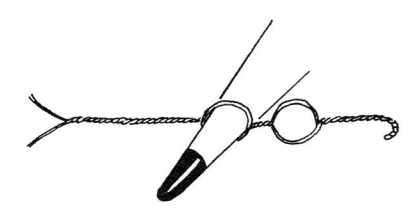

Grandma Moses

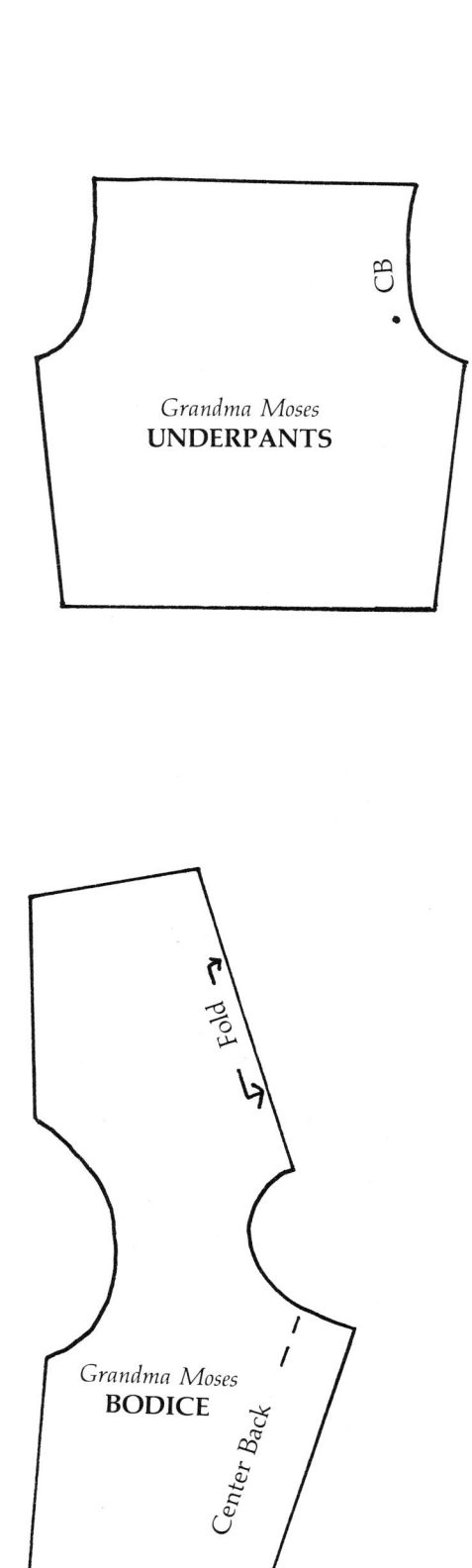

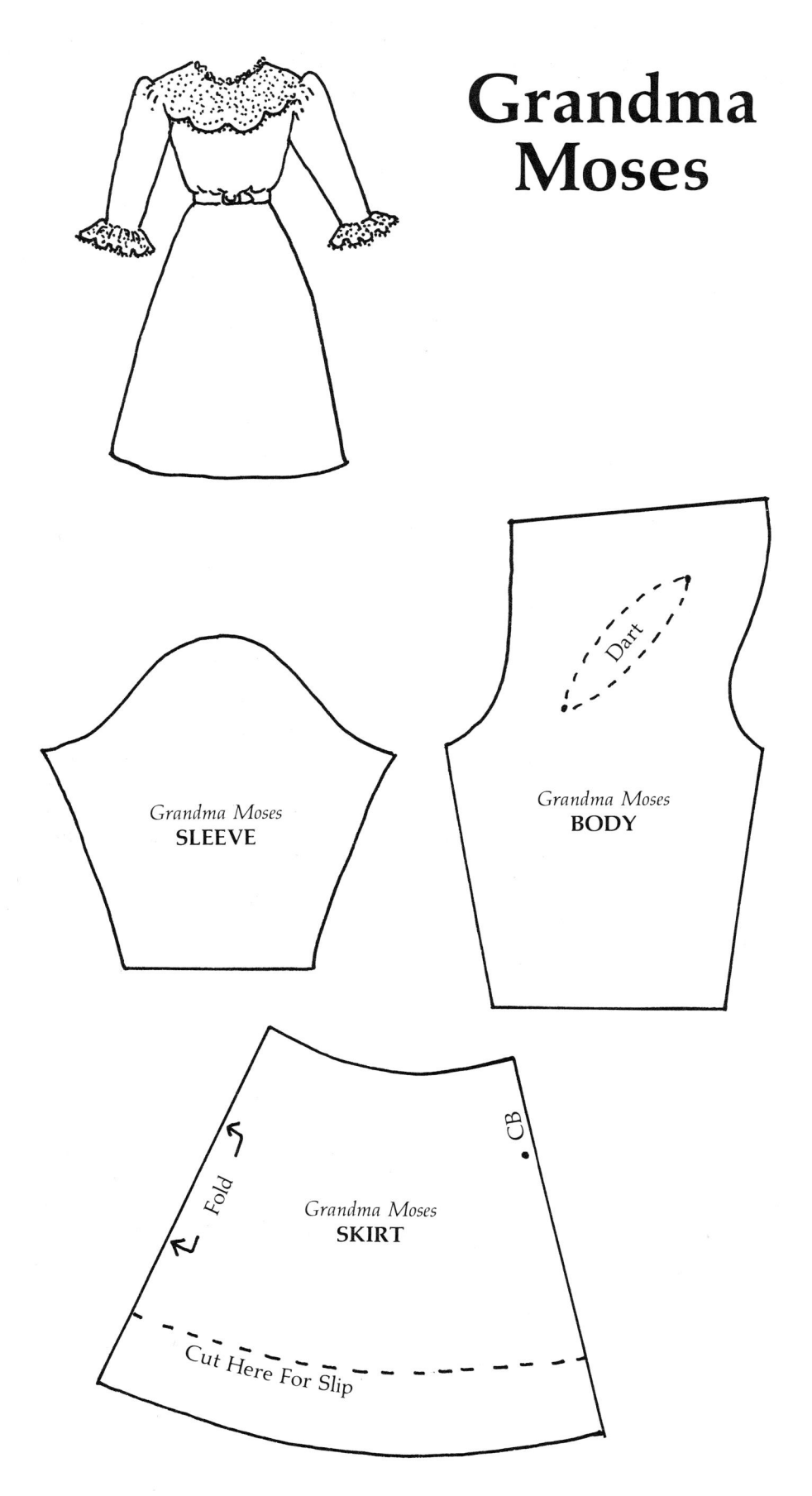

Grandma Moses
UNDERPANTS

Grandma Moses
SLEEVE

Grandma Moses
BODY

Dart

Grandma Moses
SKIRT

Fold

CB

Cut Here For Slip

Grandma Moses
BODICE

Fold

Center Back

Amelia Earhart is always the sole of femininity in her photographs. She often wore a necklace, scarf or other accessories with her flight suit.

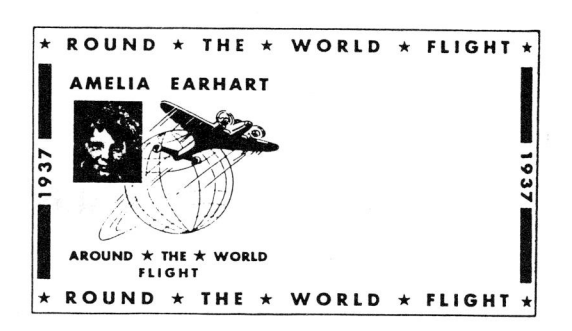

AMELIA EARHART

She was born Amelia Mary Earhart on July 24, 1898. She saw her first airplane at the Iowa State Fair in 1908. The eleven-year-old girl was not impressed.

Amelia was a slender, intense, scholarly and introverted young woman, but she was also high spirited with a sense of humor. At age 19 she entered the Ogontz School, a "female college," near Philadelphia. She joined the American Red Cross while there. Amelia left during her senior term without graduating to go to Toronto to nurse the war wounded.

In Toronto at the Exposition she saw stunt flyers. That began her obsession with flying.

Returning to the United States, she became the first woman to graduate from the Curtiss School of Aviation. She continued on to many other firsts. In June of 1928 she became the first woman to cross the Atlantic by air. In May of 1932 she became the first woman to solo across the Atlantic and the first person to cross it twice by air. In January of 1935 she became the first person to fly from Hawaii to California and the first person to fly anywhere in the Pacific. In 1937, during a round-the-world flight, Amelia Earhart's plane went down and she was lost forever to an adoring world.

FACE: Amelia had a long face with well-formed cheeks, a smallish nose and blue eyes. She was often photographed giving the world a friendly grin.

HAIR: Short hair is the most difficult to do neatly. You may want to model and paint the hair. I used pre-curled mohair on my doll. This is very tightly curled and made specifically for use on small scaled dolls.

Take two 1½in (4cm) pieces of brown curly mohair. Gently spread them out. Tie the two pieces together in the middle with matching thread. Spread and glue onto head. Let dry. Trim into short style.

CUTTING: From medium brown cotton cut two sleeves, one shirt and two pants. From dark brown velvet, short pile fur, or fleece cut one collar. The belt can be a 1/8in (0.3cm) strip of leather, felt, or grosgrain ribbon in matching brown. The scarf is a bias strip of chiffon of any pastel color.

SHIRT: Apply a thin line of glue around the neck so it does not ravel. Turn under the sleeve hems and machine stitch. Set in each sleeve by hand or machine, whichever is easiest for you. Turn under right front on dotted line. Topstitch in two rows set close together. Sew the side/underarm seams. Turn right side out and put on doll. Glue the shirt closed at the center front. Glue on the "fur" collar.

SLACKS: Fold each pant leg in half lengthwise. Topstitch along the fold line. This makes a fake side seam. Hem each pant leg by pressing the hem allowance under and machine stitch. Sew the center front seam. Sew the center back seam up to the dot. Sew the leg seam matching each pant leg at the hems and matching the center back to the center front at the crotch. Turn and put on doll. Sew up the center back seam and run a row of gathering stitches around the waist.

Make a belt buckle from lightweight brass colored wire. Try wrapping it around a needle nose pliers to get a round shape. Thread the belt through it and glue in place. Tie on the scarf.

Amelia Earhart

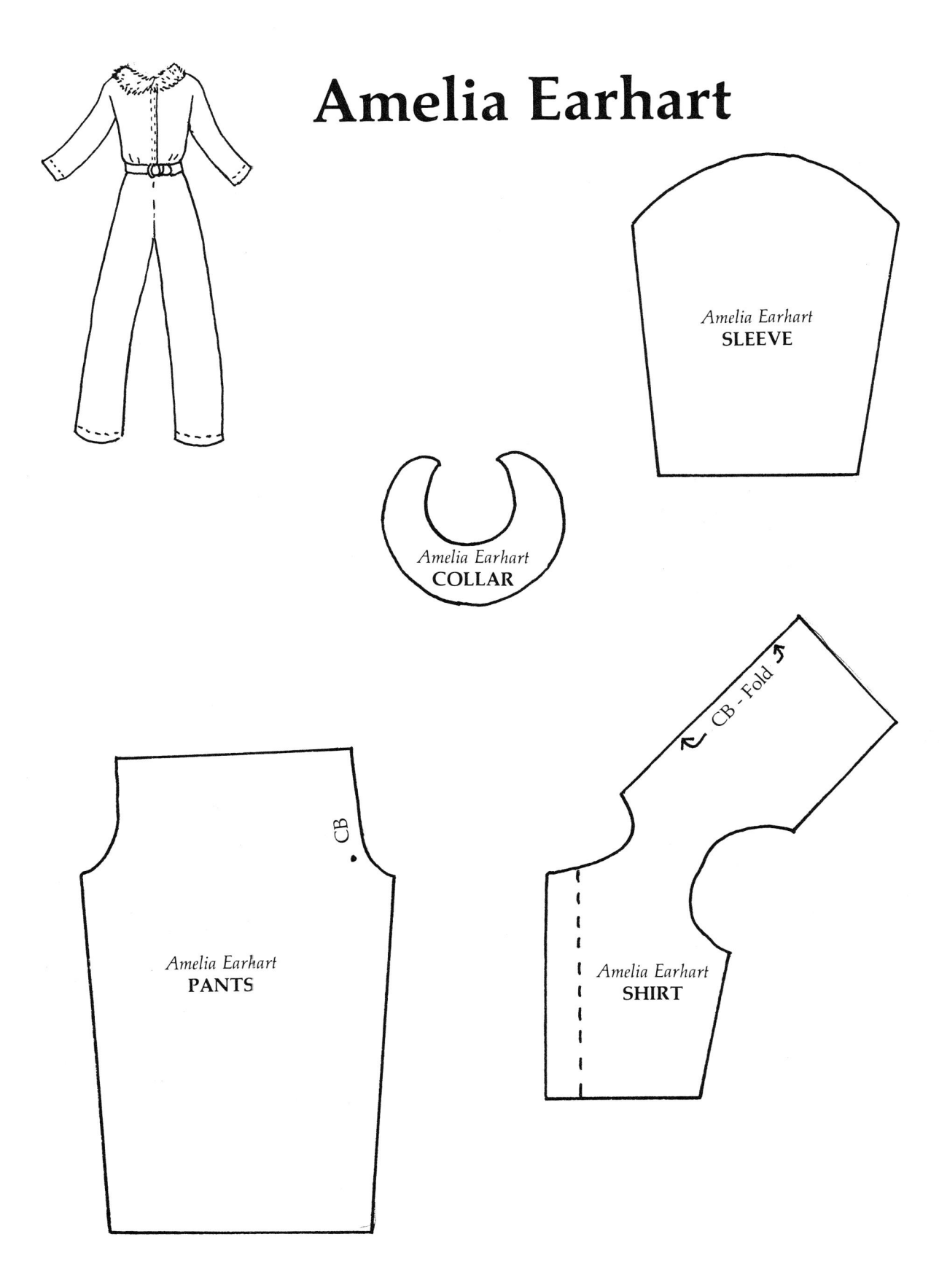

Amelia Earhart
SLEEVE

Amelia Earhart
COLLAR

Amelia Earhart
PANTS

CB

Amelia Earhart
SHIRT

CB - Fold

Mary Cassatt holds tiny brushes made from broom straws and foil. Tiny roses on the tea cart by Cindy Orwan.

MARY CASSATT

She was born Mary Stevenson Cassatt on May 22, 1845, in Allegheny City, Pennsylvania, to a prosperous well-connected family.

In 1861 Mary enrolled in the Pennsylvania Academy of Fine Arts in Philadelphia. She studied there for four years. In 1866 she embarked for Europe to continue her education by studying the Masters. In 1872 her first work was accepted by the Paris Salon, an important event that established her as a professional artist. In 1873 Mary settled in Paris. Here she formed a friendship with the artist, Edgar Degas, an Impressionist. She was the only American invited to exhibit with the Impressionists, an anti-Paris Salon reactionary group.

An accomplished artist in her own right, she was also a woman of taste who, through her wealthy American friends, was responsible for establishing fine collections of European art in America. Her work has been too lightly dismissed because she often chose domestic subject matter. This is a pity because her work is not only technically brilliant, but also a chronicle of family life in her time.

Mary Cassatt died at Mesnil-Theribus, Oise, France, June 19, 1926.

THE FACE: Mary Cassatt was a slender aristocratic woman with a long face and pointed chin. Her nose was a bit large and turned up at the end. She had gray eyes.

THE BODY: Make as in the basic body but you may wish to use muslin instead of felt for the arm tube as this style has a very slim sleeve.

THE HAIR: This wig is made from brown pre-curled mohair. A line of glue is placed around the hairline and a second line of glue is run inside the first.

The mohair is cut into two lengths of about 1¼in (3cm) and "combed" through with a large needle. Then it is pressed into place around the hairline. The tacky glue should hold it in place.

When dry, make a "pony tail" towards the back of the head using brown thread to wrap and tie it in place. Glue the ends down carefully trimming away any that are too long. Glue a black silk bow to the top of the "pony tail."

CUTTING: From white cotton cut one bodice, two sleeve tops, two sleeve bottoms, two pantalets and three skirt fronts for the slip, trimming 1/2in (1cm) off each at top.

From dark material of your choice cut one skirt front and one skirt back.

Have on hand three seed pearls for buttons, 1/8in (0.3cm) silk ribbon in white and black, 3/8in (1cm) cotton lace, 1/8in (0.3cm) grosgrain ribbon in white for belt and a little brass-colored wire for the belt buckle.

PANTALETS: Glue lace along each bottom edge. Sew the center front seam. Sew center back seam from crotch to dot. Sew the leg seam, matching the center front to the center back at the crotch. Turn. Put on doll. Sew up the center back. Gather at the waist.

SLIP: Sew the three panels together at the side seams. Press seams open. Glue lace over the bottom edge. Starting 1/2in (1cm) from the top, sew down the center back seam. Turn. Run a row of overcasting around the waist. Leave enough thread at the beginning and end to gather and knot. Place slip on doll. Sew up the center back seam. Pull the overcasting tight and knot thread. Use a dot of glue to hold the knot.

BLOUSE: Press under one sleeve bottom on the dotted line. Do the opposite side on the other sleeve bottom. Glue lace along each cuff. Glue a sleeve bottom on each of the doll's arms. The folded edge will cover the raw edge and make a glued seam. Place the seams where they would ordinarily occur on a sewn blouse.

Run a line of glue around the neckline so it does not fray. Let dry. Sew 1/8in (0.3cm) ribbon around the neckline by hand using tiny stitches.

Gather the sleeve tops along the curved edge and set in the armholes of the bodice. Sew in place by hand using small stitches and adjusting the gathers evenly as you sew.

Turn under the raw edge on each sleeve top. Gather with small stitches and knot.

SKIRT: Sew skirt front to skirt back at the side seams. Hem. Place on doll. Gather at the waist and knot.

FINISHING: Take 12in (31cm) of lace and glue the ends together being sure that it is not twisted. Gather using an overcast stitch.

Make a line of glue where the lace should go. (See dotted line on pattern.) Glue ruffle in place, adjusting the gathers before the glue dries.

Glue a small silk bow at the collar and three small seed pearl "buttons" down the front.

From wire, using a small needle nose pliers, bend a buckle. (See diagram.) Thread the grosgrain ribbon through the buckle and trim to make a belt. Glue in place.

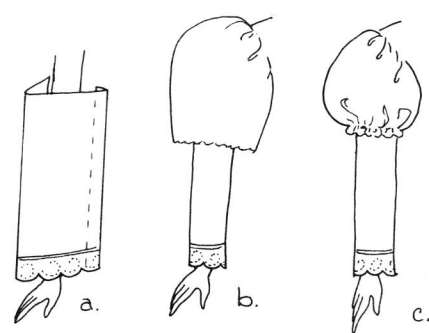

SLEEVE DETAIL

a. Shows the arm tube. The dotted line represents the turned under edge of the sleeve bottom.

b. The bodice and upper sleeve are put on the doll.

c. The raw edge is turned under and gathered by hand.

Mary Cassatt

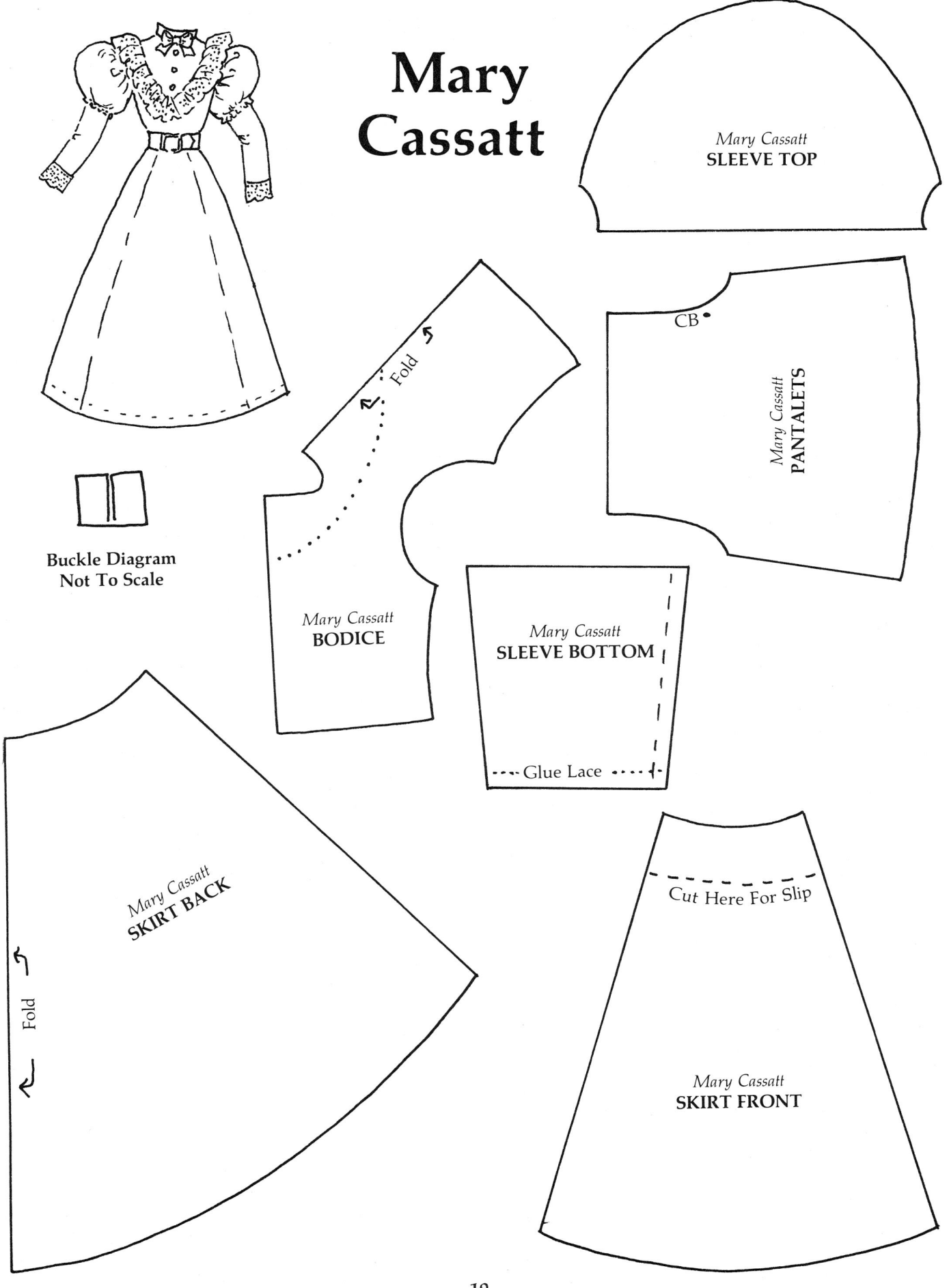

Mary Cassatt **SLEEVE TOP**

Buckle Diagram Not To Scale

Fold

Mary Cassatt **BODICE**

CB

Mary Cassatt **PANTALETS**

Mary Cassatt **SLEEVE BOTTOM**

Glue Lace

Mary Cassatt **SKIRT BACK**

Fold

Cut Here For Slip

Mary Cassatt **SKIRT FRONT**

19

*Ladies of **Mercy Otis Warren's** day wore lace caps when at home. The flowers are made from Sculpey. The brass watering can is an almost-antique piece.*

MERCY OTIS WARREN

Mercy Otis, born in 1728, was the third of thirteen children born to a prominent Cape Cod family. She was trained in all the feminine arts and also allowed to study with her brothers under the tutelage of a local pastor, the learned Johnathon Russell. She was an excellent student.

Through her favorite brother, James Otis, Junior or Jemmy as the family called him, she met James Warren. They were an ideal couple, sympathetic in politics, of similar background, and educated. They were married in 1754.

Jemmy was always a large influence on Mercy's life. He was an active patriot, an eloquent orator for the cause and a writer of influence. Unfortunately, by 1769 he had pushed himself too far and had a nervous breakdown. He never recovered.

In the early 1770s Mercy took up her pen at the suggestion of John Adams, a family friend, and began writing for the cause. Certainly she realized that she was picking up the banner that Jemmy had dropped.

She began with some poems but soon struck on the idea of writing satire. Her satirical plays, "The Adulateur: A Tragedy; As It Is Now Acted In Upper Servia" and "The Group," were much read in the colonies.

Her greatest achievement was her three-volume set entitled *History of the Rise, Progress, and Termination of the American Revolution* published in Boston in 1805.

Mercy Otis Warren, faithful wife, good mother, loving sister, and historian of the American Revolution died in 1814.

FACE: Mercy had a long aristocratic face, straight nose, wide mouth and brown eyes.

HAIR: Use either mohair or brown acrylic fiber (sold under the name Feel O' Fleece). Pull off a small piece about 4in (10cm) long and 3/4in (2cm) wide. Lay on paper and sew through the middle to form a part. Gently tear away the paper. Glue to head, spreading to cover. When the glue dries, twist the ends into a low bun. Glue in place.

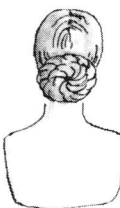

CUTTING: From white cotton cut a piece 3in (8cm) by 8in (20cm) for the slip. From a lightweight solid fabric cut one bodice insert, a piece 3¾in (10cm) by 10in (25cm) for an underskirt, two sleeves, two overskirt fronts, one overdress, and two sleeve ruffles (using the pattern piece marked "fabric"). From white lace or tulle cut two sleeve ruffles using pattern piece marked lace.

Have on hand 22in (56cm) of lace that coordinates with or matches the dress fabric. Width does not matter as it may be trimmed but it should have a dainty pattern on the scalloped edge. Also have 20in (51cm) of fancy trim to be glued on the center front edges of the overdress, white bunka, and 5/8in (2cm) lace to make the slip ruffle.

SLIP: Turn up and hem. Sew or glue the center back seam. Gather 20in (51cm) of lace and glue to slip to form ruffle. The ruffle should extend a little below the hem. Gather with the overcast stitch. Slip on doll and secure.

BODICE INSERT: Make a lace-finished edge on the top of the bodice insert. To do this, on the right side of your fabric place your lace fancy side down (toward the waist in this case). Sew through close to the scalloped edge. Turn the lace to the back and press. Topstitch to hold in place. Glue the bodice insert to the doll.

OVERSKIRT: Turn up hem and sew. Sew center back and press open. Gather with overcast stitch. Slip on doll and secure tightly in place.

OVERDRESS: Right sides out, match the center back at the dots and stitch on the dotted line. Fold the back of the dress into four pleats as shown in illustration. Topstitch in place by hand, using small stitches.

Join the overskirt fronts to the bodice on the dotted lines. Each skirt front should be arranged in three graceful pleats. Hand sew, using small stitches. Make a lace-finished edge (see above) up one center front, around the neck and down the opposite center front.

Run a thin line of glue along the lower edge of each sleeve so it will not ravel. Sew a sleeve in each armhole. Sew the side/sleeve seams. Turn. Press under the hem and stitch in place. Put dress on doll and tack at the center front of the waist.

Glue unraveled bunka around the outside edges of all four sleeve ruffles. Run a row of overcast stitches around the inside opening of one of the fabric sleeve ruffles. Put on doll and pull up over the sleeve. Do not glue yet!

Run a row of overcast stitches around the inside opening of a lace ruffle. Run a line of glue around the bottom of the sleeve. Gather the lace ruffle and press in place on the row of glue. Let dry. The longest part of the ruffle should fall down the back of the arm.

Run a row of glue around the sleeve at the top of the lace ruffle. Gather the fabric ruffle and glue in place. Let dry. Glue a row of unraveled bunka around the top of the fabric ruffle.

Glue fancy trim up one center front of the overdress, around the neck and down the opposite center front.

HAT: Gather the hat by hand. Glue in place on the doll's head. Gather a dainty lace ruffle and glue around the hat. Add a bow in the back, if you wish, leaving long dangly ends.

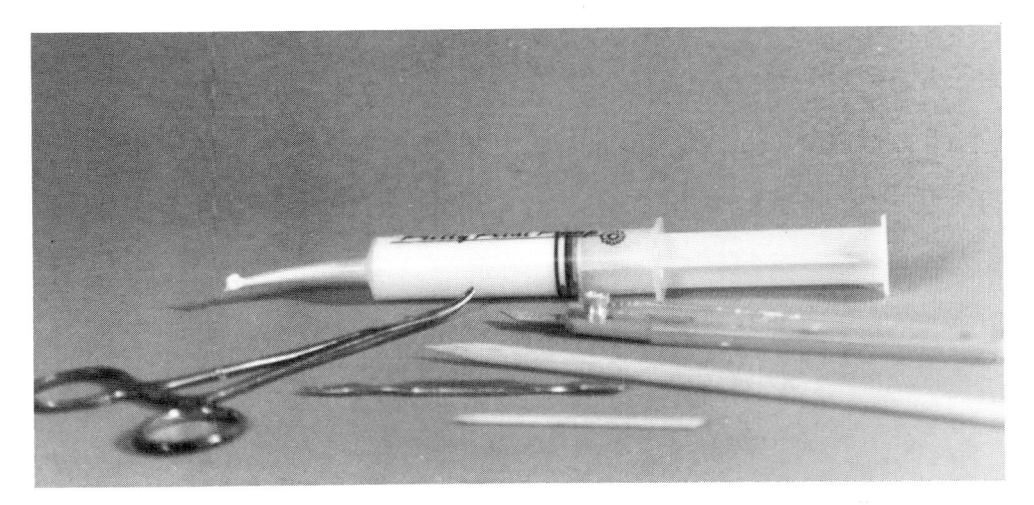

Illustration 3.
Some tools I find useful, starting at the top and going clockwise, a glue gun or syringe, a craft knife, an orange stick, a toothpick, a manicure tool and a hemostat or forceps.

Illustration 4.
Using the toothpick, orange stick and manicure tool, the parts for the Mercy Otis Warren doll are here shown modeled.

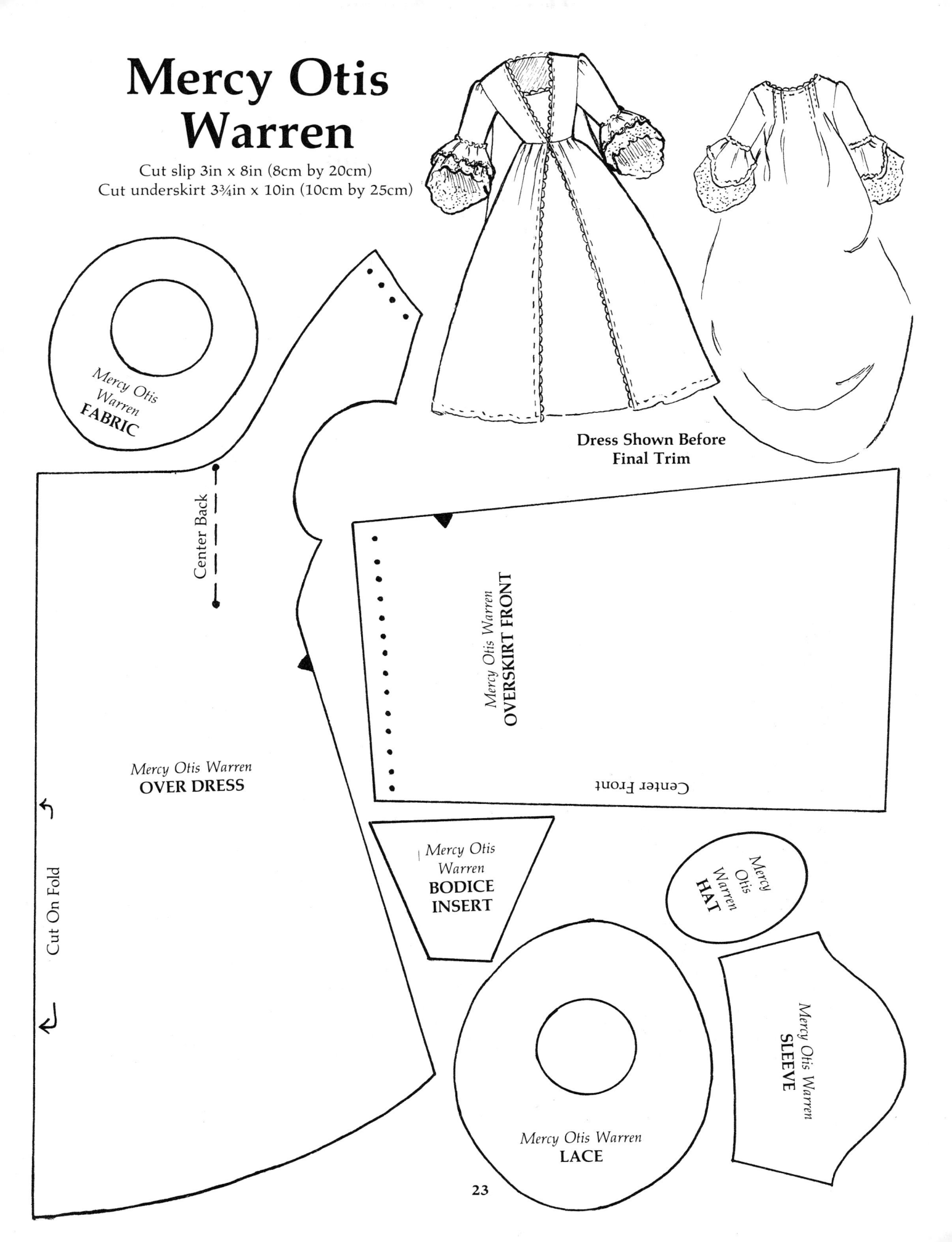

Mercy Otis Warren

Cut slip 3in x 8in (8cm by 20cm)
Cut underskirt 3¾in x 10in (10cm by 25cm)

Dress Shown Before Final Trim

Mercy Otis Warren **FABRIC**

Center Back

Mercy Otis Warren **OVER DRESS**

Cut On Fold

Mercy Otis Warren **OVERSKIRT FRONT**

Center Front

Mercy Otis Warren **BODICE INSERT**

Mercy Otis Warren **HAT**

Mercy Otis Warren **LACE**

Mercy Otis Warren **SLEEVE**

***Margaret Sanger** in her visiting nurse's uniform gives advice to a new mother. Wicker chair by Donna Stalter.*

MARGARET SANGER

Many people encounter social wrongs but few have the courage to try to change them. Margaret Sanger was such a woman. Born Maggie Higgins on September 14, 1883, she was one of eleven children. In addition, her mother suffered seven miscarriages.

As the young Maggie watched her tuburcular mother grow weaker and weaker with each pregnancy, she became angry. She noticed that only the poor in her town had large families. The wealthy seemed able to limit their families. What was their secret?

She attended Claverack College where she took the more dignified name of Margaret. She was unable to finish college as she was called home to nurse her dying mother.

After trying her hand at teaching for two years, she left to study nursing. While a nurse probationer, she met William Sanger, an architect and radical thinker. They were married. After marriage she worked for the Visiting Nurse Association. Everywhere she looked the story was the same. Impoverished women, sick and weakened from many pregnancies, would beg her to tell them the "secret". At that time it was illegal even for a doctor to give birth control advice to a married woman.

Margaret decided to take on the Comstock Law by publishing and distributing birth control information. Although she was often arrested and sometimes thrown into jail, through her persistence, she was able to gradually influence public opinion.

She opened the first birth control clinic in the United States, published the Birth Control Review, established the Birth Control League, and organized several international conferences.

As a result of her international fame, she was invited by the Kaizo group to speak in Japan as part of a panel that consisted of herself, Albert Einstein, Bertrand Russell, and H. G. Wells. In 1936, largely because of her persistent years of effort, the law was changed to allow doctors to dispense birth control.

In 1931, she was awarded the Medal of Honor by the American Women's Association. It bore the citation:

for integrity, valor and honor...for fighting her battle single-handed, a pioneer of pioneers. She has opened the door of knowledge and given light, freedom and happiness to thousands caught in the tragic meshes of ignorance. She is remaking the world.

Margaret Sanger died in 1966.

FACE: Margaret Sanger was always described as a beautiful and feminine woman. She had soft features and hazel eyes.

HAIR: Using red mohair or acrylic fiber, pull off small pieces and comb through them with a large needle. Lay them out on a sheet of paper and sew through the mohair. Pull away the paper. You should now have a long strip of mohair.

Run a line of glue around the hairline. Run a second row of glue inside the first. Press the mohair onto the glue. The sewn edge should go around at the hairline. The long ends of the mohair should hang down. When the glue dries, pull the mohair up as if you were making a ponytail, but instead twist the ends into a bun. Glue in place.

CUTTING: From lightweight iron-on innerfacing cut one apron shape. Iron it onto white cotton. Cut the cotton 3/16in (0.5cm) larger than the innerfacing all around. From white cotton also cut two pantalets and a slip 2¾in (7cm) by 6in (15cm).

From blue (I used a small blue and white stripe) cut one bodice and a skirt 3¼in (8cm) by 9in (23cm). Cut a strip from the selvage for a belt.

Have on hand some narrow white lace, some 1/8in (0.3cm) white ribbon for the apron, and a small amount of 1/8in (0.3cm) burgundy ribbon for her tie.

Visiting Nurse Uniform

PANTALETS: Glue lace along each bottom edge. Sew the center front seam. Sew the center back seam from crotch to dot. Sew the leg seam, matching the center back to the center front at the crotch. Turn. Put on doll. Sew up the center back. Gather at the waist.

SLIP: Glue lace along the bottom edge. Glue closed at the center back. Run a row of overcast gathering stitches around the waist. Put on doll. Pull tight. Knot. Are you using a dot of glue to set your knots?

BODICE: Run a row of glue around the neckline and let dry. Sew white ribbon around the neck to make a stand up collar. Glue white ribbon or a selvage strip from your white cotton around each wrist of the doll to form cuffs. Sew the underarm/side seams. Turn. Place bodice on doll and sew closed at the center back. Turn under the bottom of each sleeve and gather with an overstitch. The white "cuffs" should show at the bottom.

SKIRT: Glue a 1/4in (0.7cm) hem along the bottom. Glue the center back closed. Gather the skirt with a small running stitch. Put the skirt on the doll. Pull tight. Knot. Cover the waist with a waistband made from the selvage edge of your blue material.

APRON: Press the seam allowance over and glue down. Sew two pieces of white ribbon to the sides for ties. Place the apron on the doll and glue a small piece of white ribbon in place for the neck strap.

Glue a burgundy bow in place at the neck.

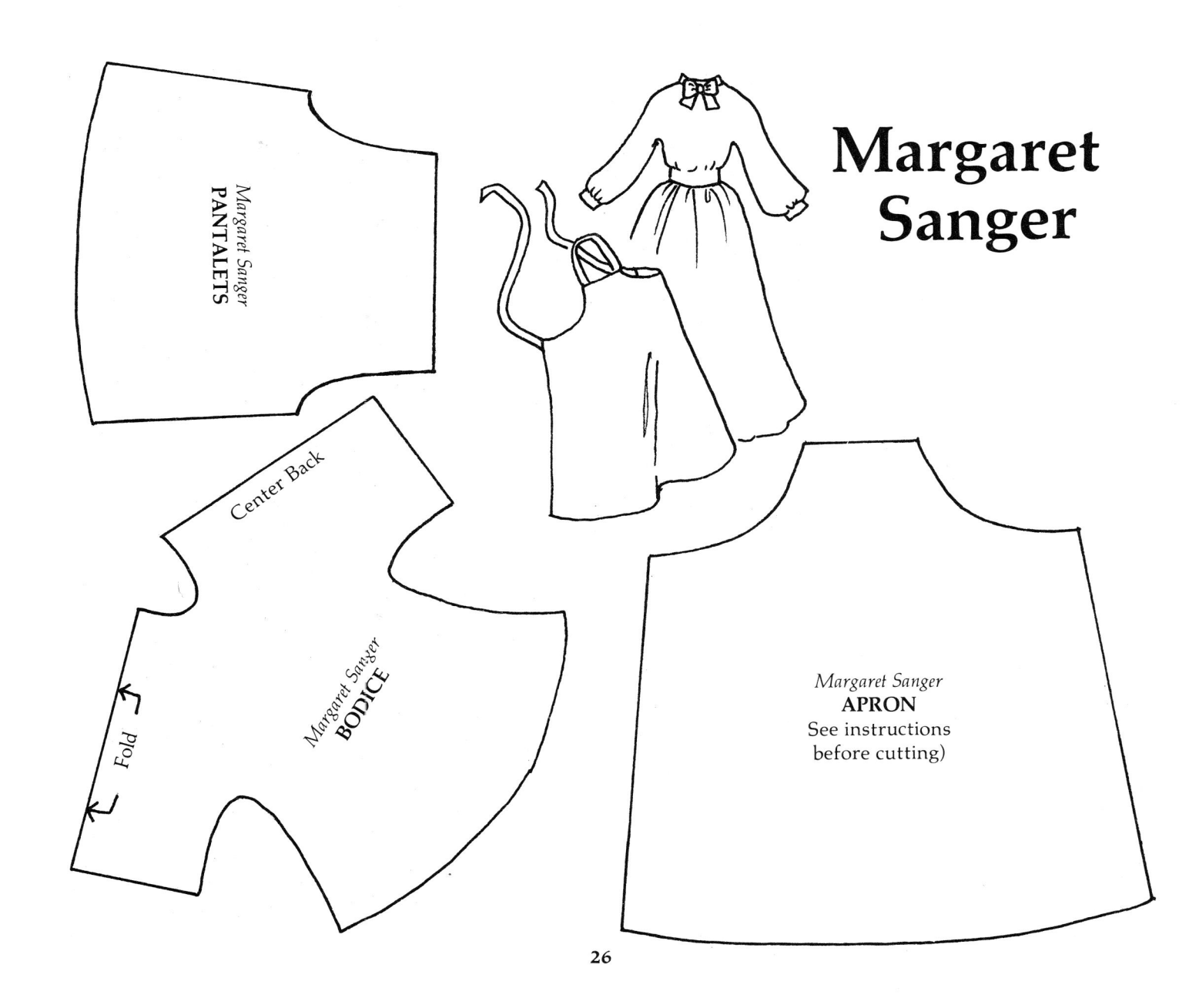

Margaret Sanger

Margaret Sanger
PANTALETS

Center Back

Fold

Margaret Sanger
BODICE

Margaret Sanger
APRON
See instructions
before cutting)

Harriet Tubman's *dress was probably pieced in the skirt for utility rather than style. When dresses involved a great deal of fabric, they were repaired more often than discarded. Fireplace by George Baker.*

HARRIET TUBMAN

Born into slavery in Dorchester County, Maryland, about 1821, Harriet Tubman suffered the unhappy life of a slave. She was not educated, but rather put to work as a field hand at an early age. In 1844, she was forced by her owner to marry John Tubman, a fellow slave.

In 1849, she escaped to the North. She made 20 trips back to the South to help other slaves escape including her parents. She carried a gun or a rifle as protection against slave owners and to discourage anyone who considered turning back. Despite the fact that the Southern States had put a price of $40,000 on her head, she was able to help over 300 slaves escape.

During the Civil War Harriet worked as a scout, cook, nurse, and a spy. She founded the Harriet Tubman Home for Needy Negros. Biographer Sarah Bradford called her "the Moses of Her People."

Harriet Tubman died in 1913.

FACE: Harriet had a broad nose and full lips set in a stern expression. She had well-formed cheek bones tapering down to a narrow jaw.

HAIR: Make the wig the same as Mercy Otis Warren's. Use black mohair or fiber.

CUTTING: Cut the underwear from white cotton using the instructions from Margaret Sanger's pattern. Cut from gold cotton: one bodice, two sleeves, one lower back bodice, skirt piece A, and skirt piece C. Cut from a contrasting fabric skirt piece B. Have on hand lace for the collar and underwear, and three tiny pearls for buttons.

UNDERWEAR: Assemble, using the instructions from Margaret Sanger's pattern.

SKIRT: Fold piece C in half lengthwise. Sew to piece B (the folded edge of piece C forms the hem). Sew piece A to piece B/C. Sew the center back seam. Gather around the top using the overcast stitch. Put on doll. Fasten snugly.

BODICE: Run a line of glue around the edge of the neckline so it does not ravel. Gather the lower bodice back and sew to the bodice. Gather the sleeves slightly and set in place. You may hand-stitch them in place using tiny stitches. Turn under the sleeve hems and glue in place. Sew the side/sleeve seams. Turn under the hem and glue in place. This is a bit tricky because of the ruffle in back. Use the tip of your iron and do a little at a time.

Turn under the bodice's right center front and glue. Clip the left center front at the dot. Turn under the allowance from the dot down and glue in place.

Put the bodice on the doll. Glue closed at front. Glue lace around the neck. For the frill make a half bow. Glue it at the center front of the neckline. The tails should form a little upside-down "V". Pull the loop down and glue it in place. Glue the three bead "buttons" in place as shown.

Harriet Tubman

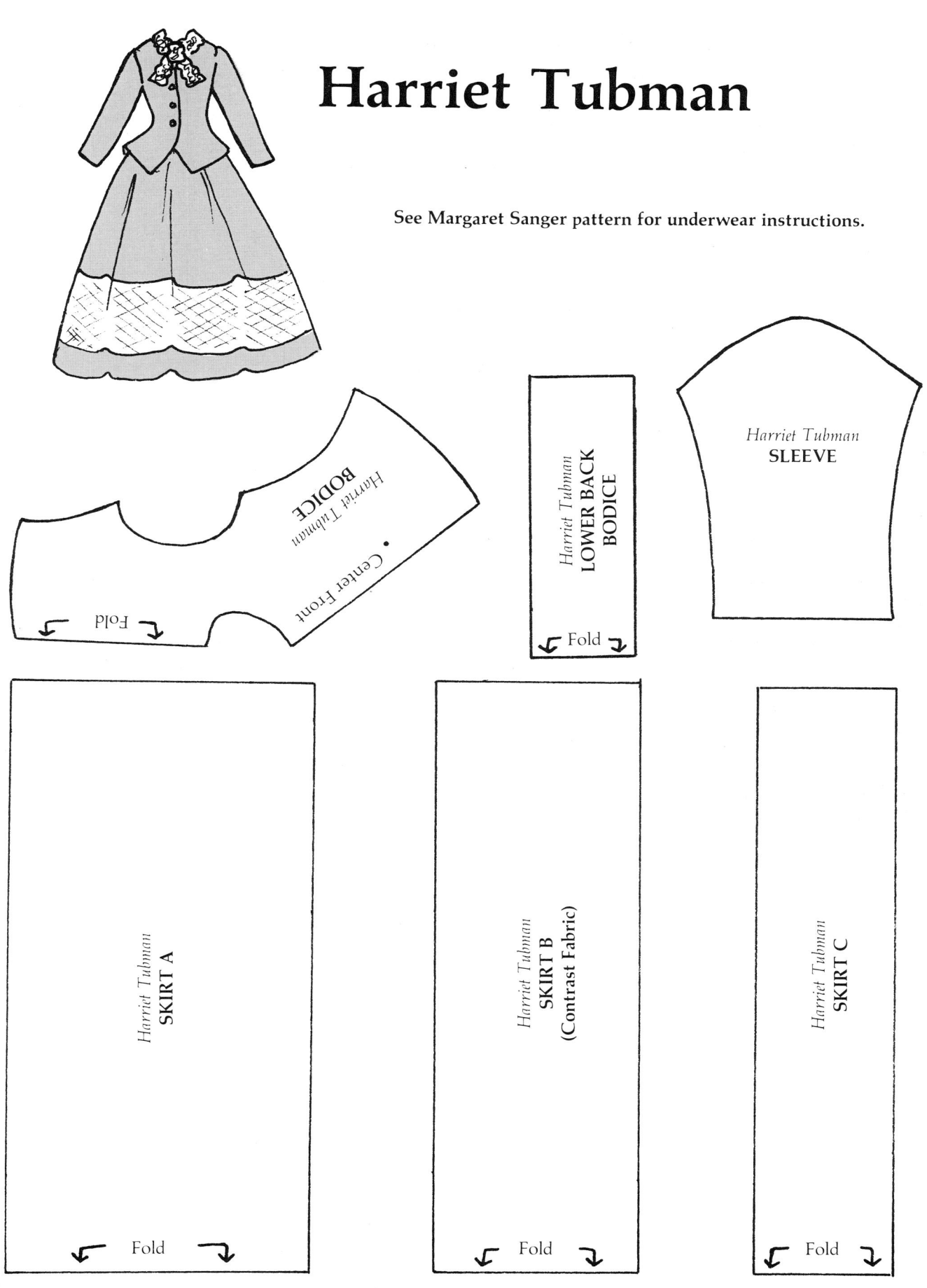

See Margaret Sanger pattern for underwear instructions.

Harriet Tubman **BODICE** · Center Front — Fold

Harriet Tubman **LOWER BACK BODICE** — Fold

Harriet Tubman **SLEEVE**

Harriet Tubman **SKIRT A** — Fold

Harriet Tubman **SKIRT B** (Contrast Fabric) — Fold

Harriet Tubman **SKIRT C** — Fold

29

Where To Buy Supplies

If you live in a small town, the hardest part of doll making could be finding supplies. Non-shrinking clays like Sculpey and Fimo, pipe cleaners, and liquid acrylic paints are available in craft stores and from craft supply catalogs.

Wire for armatures, tiny glasses and other accessories can be bought at the hardware store. Look for soft fabrics that will drape well and tiny prints at your local fabric store I buy 1/4yd (20cm) pieces when I shop and "stock pile."

Cotton lace, silk ribbons, fancy trims, glue guns and mohair can be mail ordered through businesses that advertise in **Nutshell News** and **Doll Reader®.**

Look to doll supply and miniature supply catalogs for mohair, acrylic wig fiber, doll stands and small scale accessories. Persist and you will find several sources for those special needs.

Large Size Patterns

The large size patterns are provided for those who wish to work in a larger scale. The dolls will be about 8in (20.3cm) tall.

The patterns are exactly 50% larger than the inch to the foot patterns. **Remember to allow for extra trims and fabric.**

Large Body Patterns

The head pattern is used for all dolls. The short limbs are used with the felt body No. 1 or with the wrapped wire body. The long limbs are used for felt body No. 2. All limbs should have a hole in the center to insert wire.

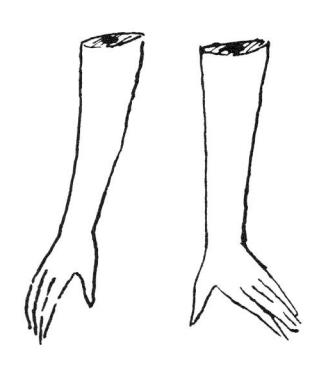

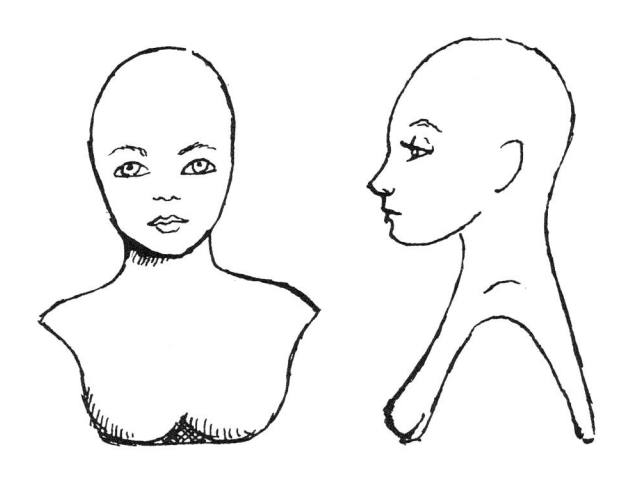

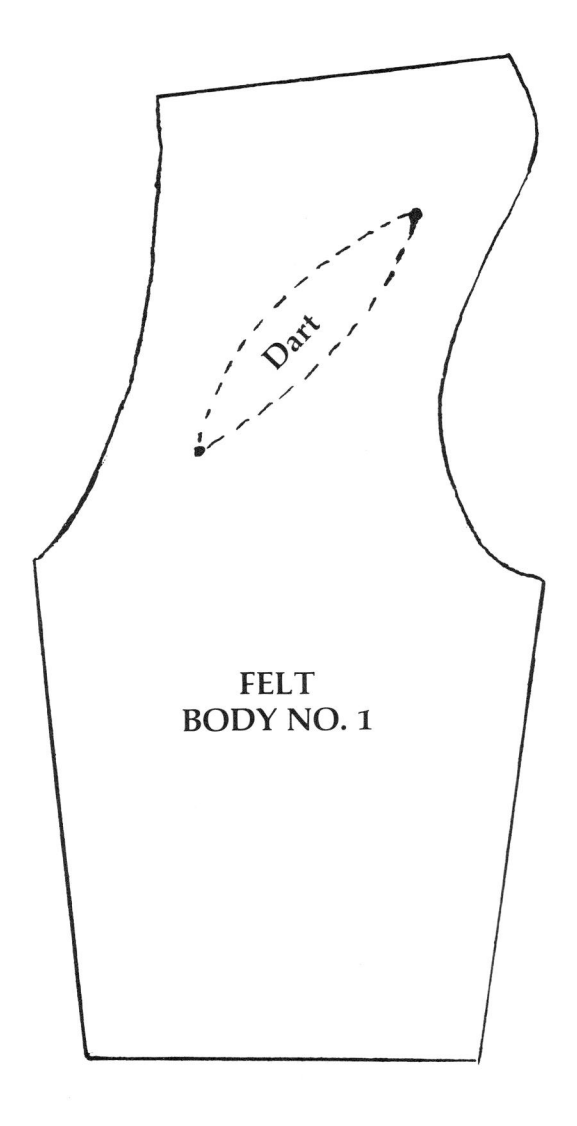

FELT BODY NO. 1

Dart

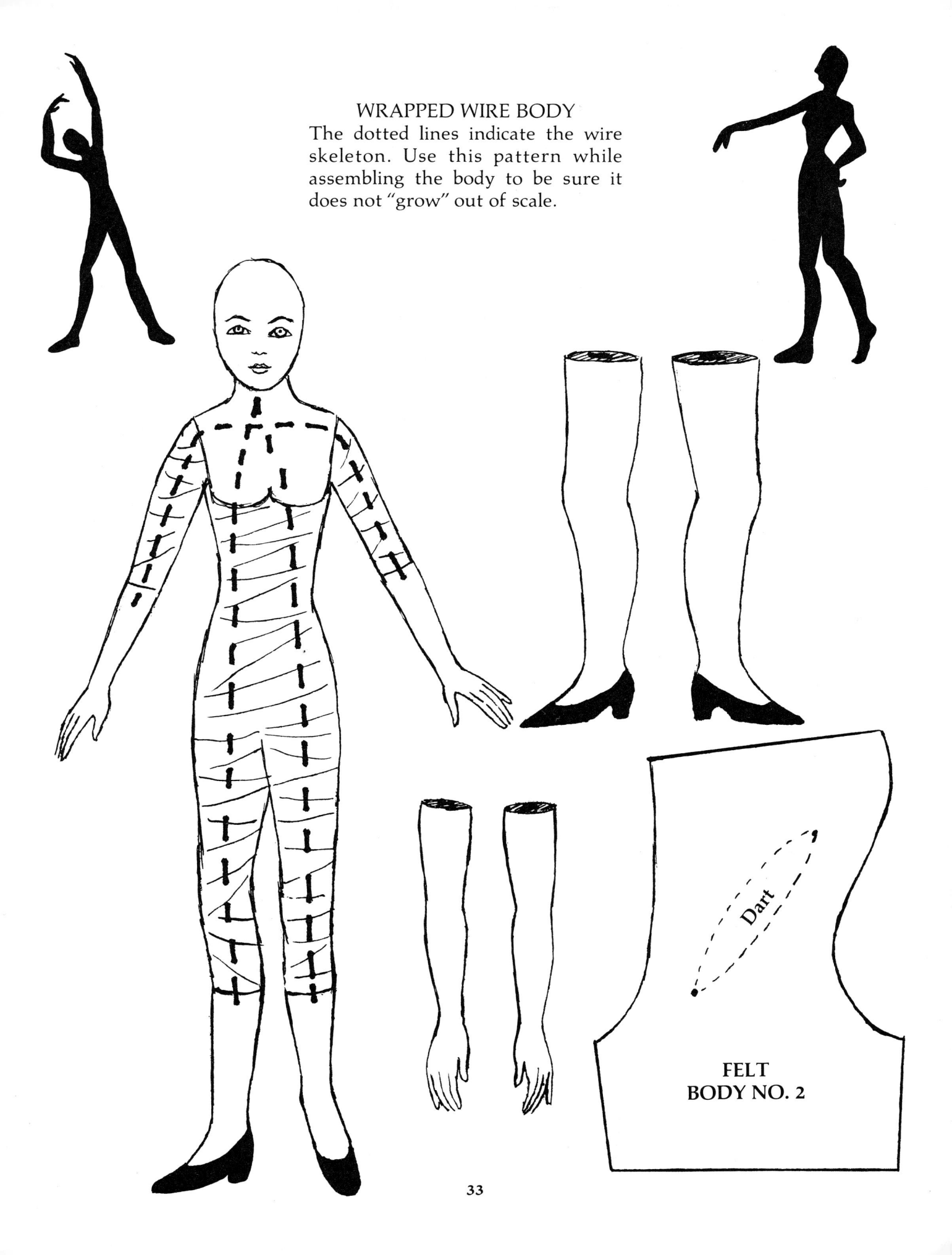

WRAPPED WIRE BODY
The dotted lines indicate the wire skeleton. Use this pattern while assembling the body to be sure it does not "grow" out of scale.

Dart

FELT
BODY NO. 2

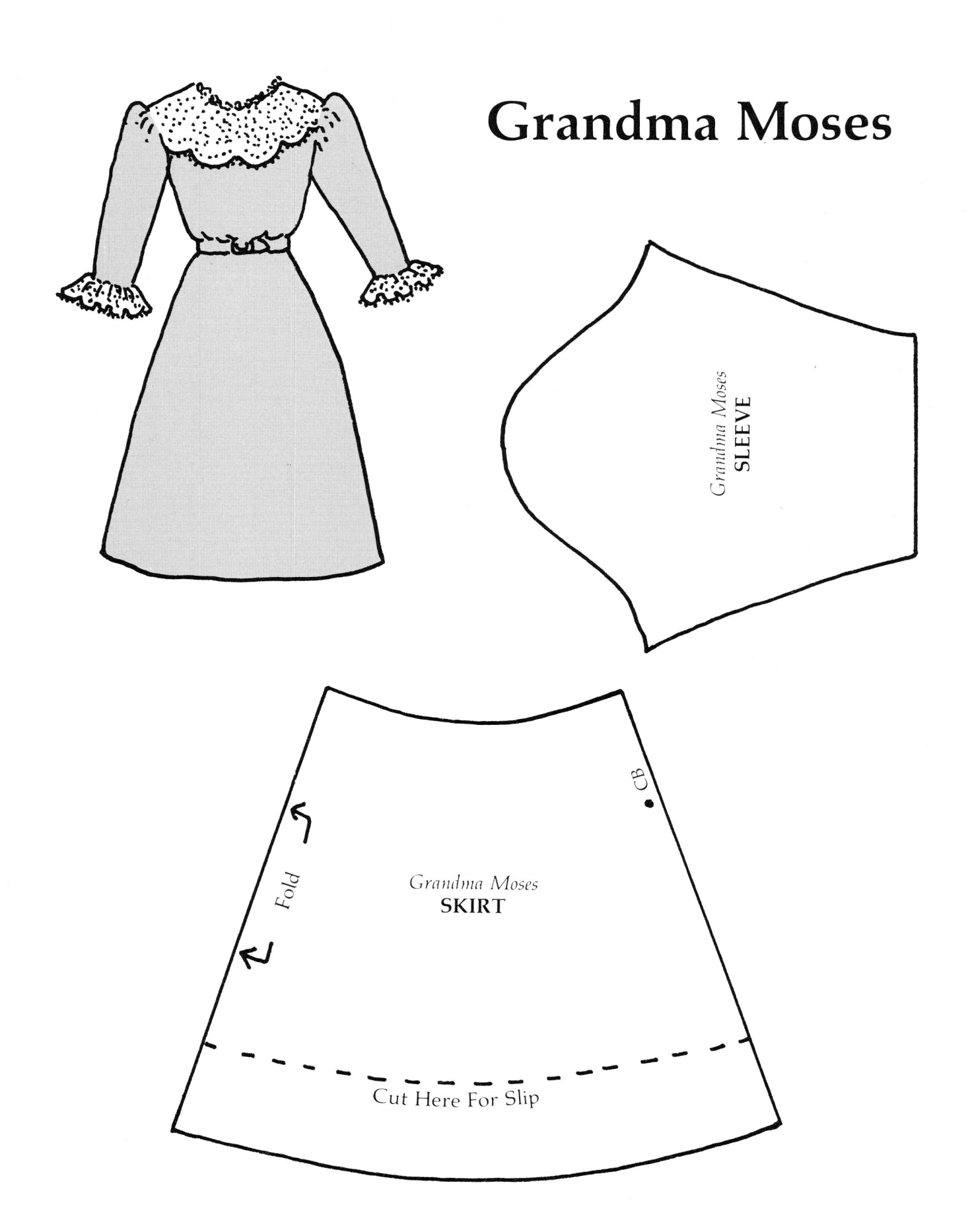

Grandma Moses

Grandma Moses
SLEEVE

Fold

Grandma Moses
SKIRT

CB

Cut Here For Slip

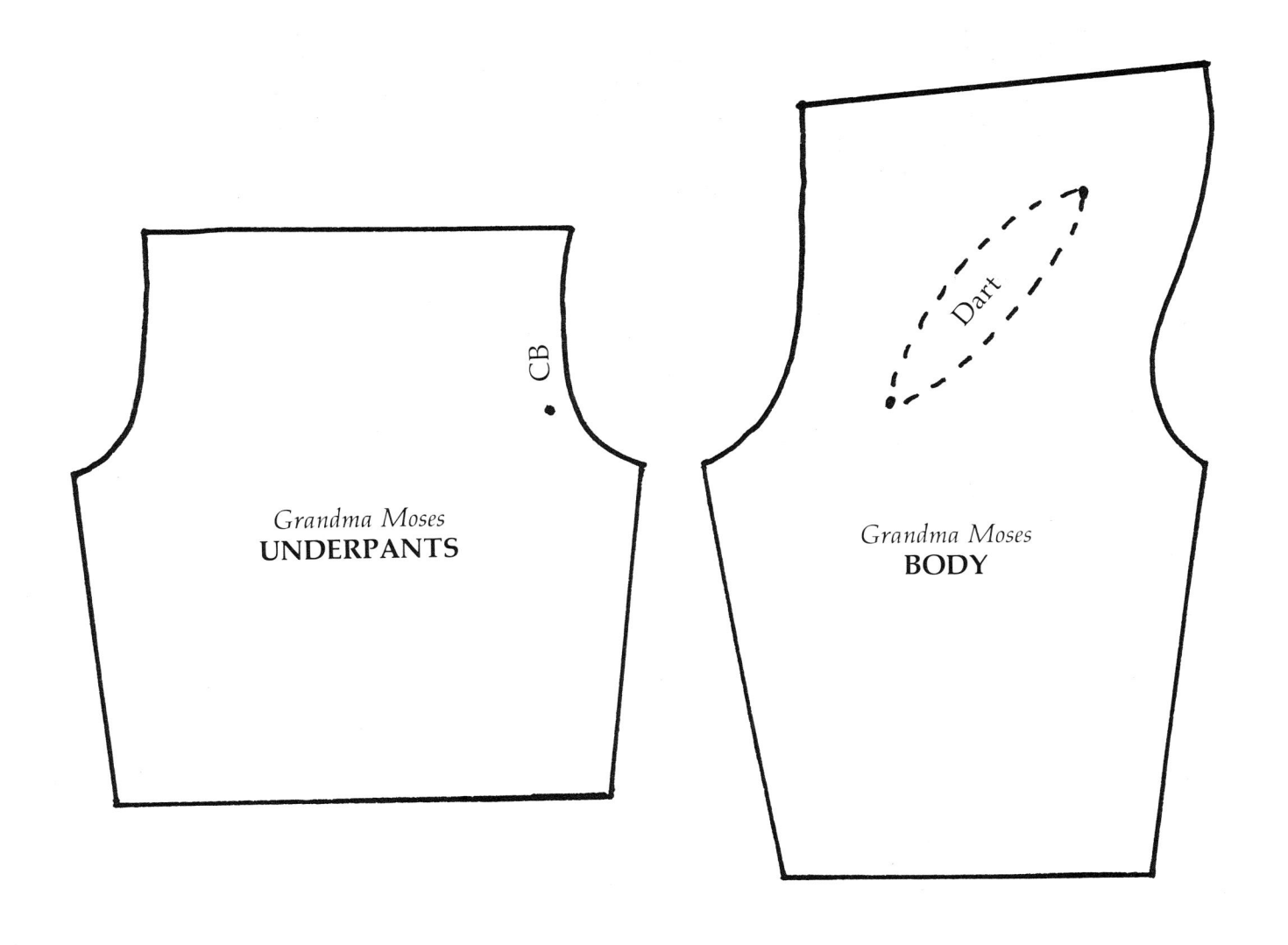

Grandma Moses
UNDERPANTS

• CB

Grandma Moses
BODY

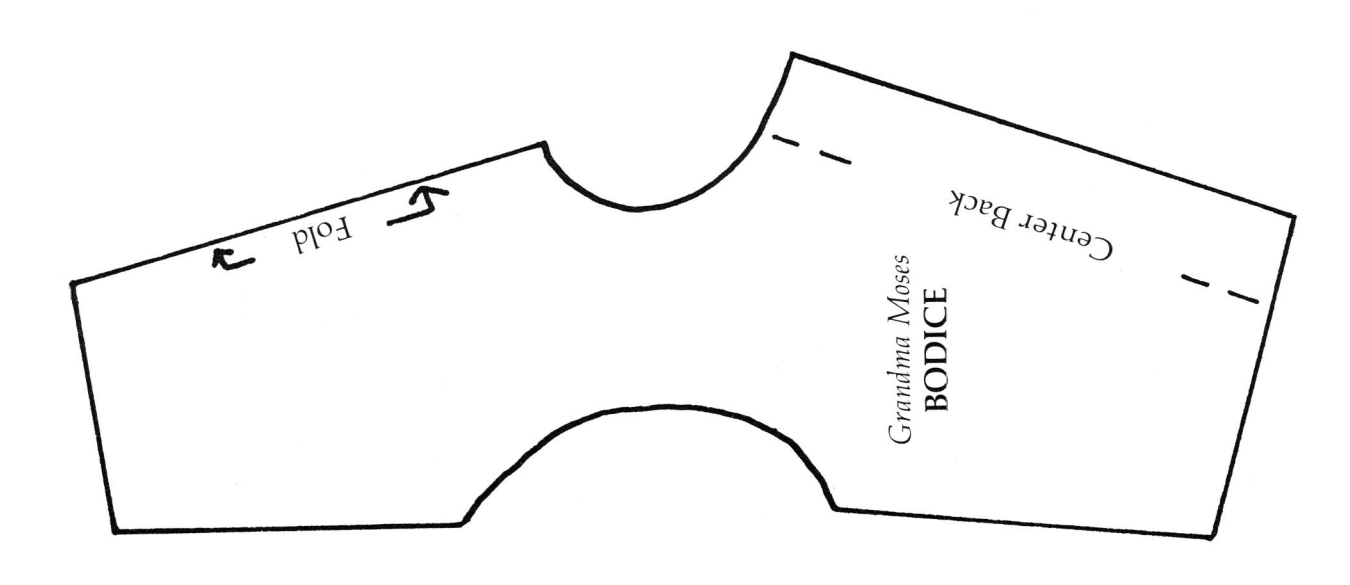

Dart

Grandma Moses
BODICE

Fold

Center Back

Amelia Earhart

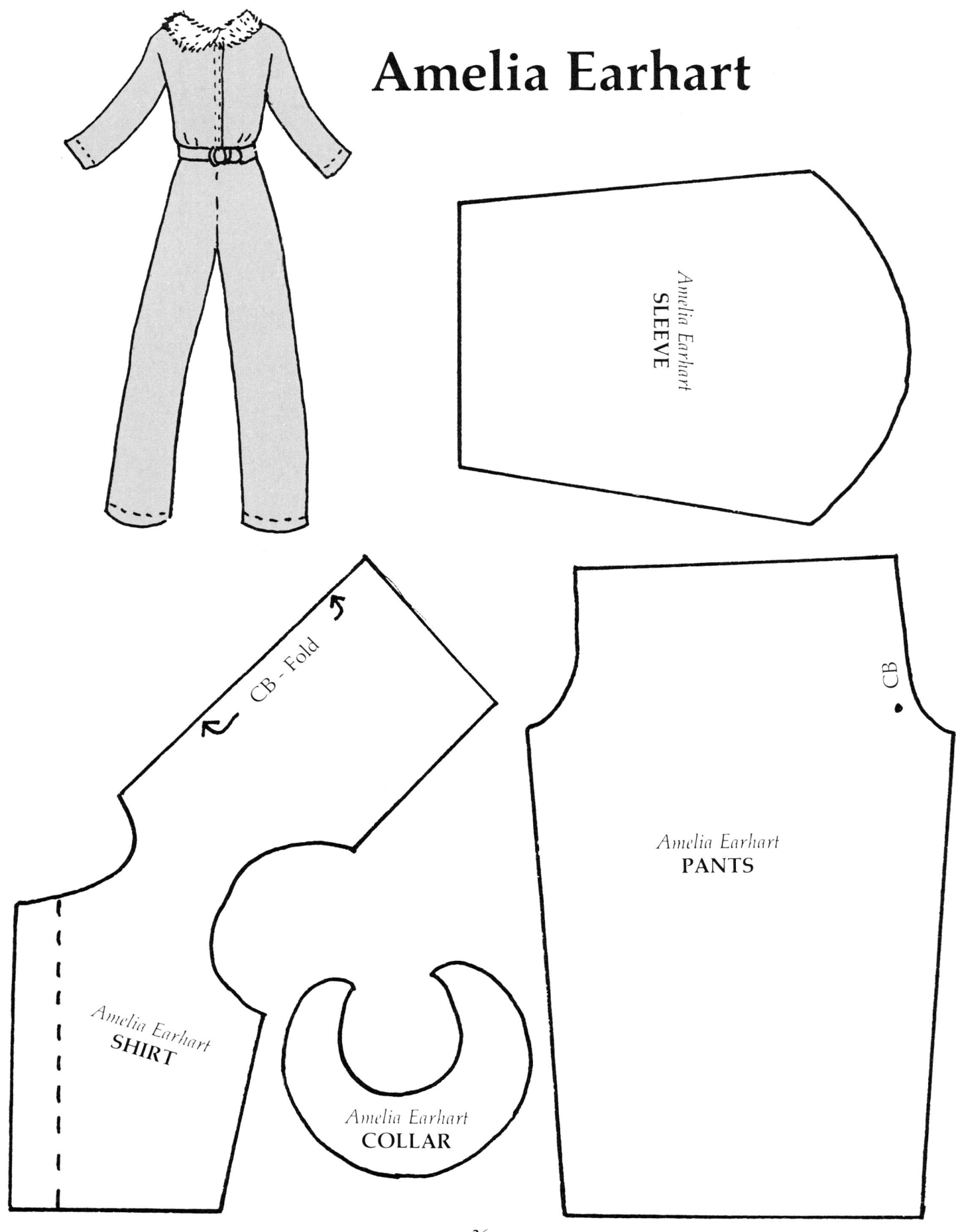

Amelia Earhart
SLEEVE

CB - Fold

Amelia Earhart
SHIRT

Amelia Earhart
COLLAR

CB

Amelia Earhart
PANTS

Mary Cassatt

Mary Cassatt
PANTALETS

• CB

Mary Cassatt
SLEEVE TOP

Cut Here For Slip

Mary Cassatt
SKIRT FRONT

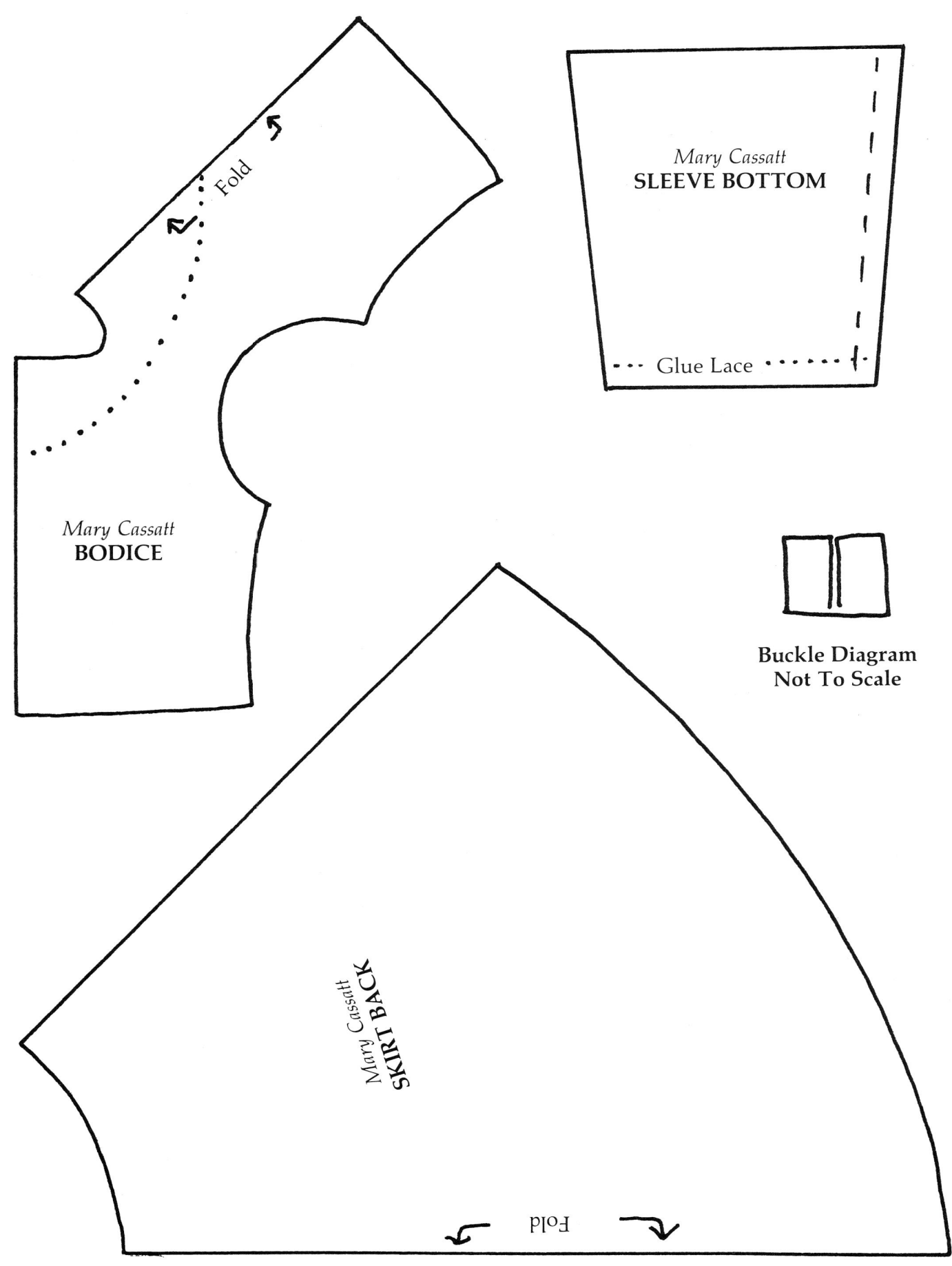

Mary Cassatt
SLEEVE BOTTOM

··· Glue Lace ···

Fold

Mary Cassatt
BODICE

**Buckle Diagram
Not To Scale**

Mary Cassatt
SKIRT BACK

Fold

Mercy Otis Warren

Dress Shown Before
Final Trim

Cut slip 4½in by 12in (12cm by 31cm)
Cut underskirt 5⅝in by 15in (14cm by 38cm)

Center Back

Cut On Fold

Mercy Otis Warren
OVER DRESS

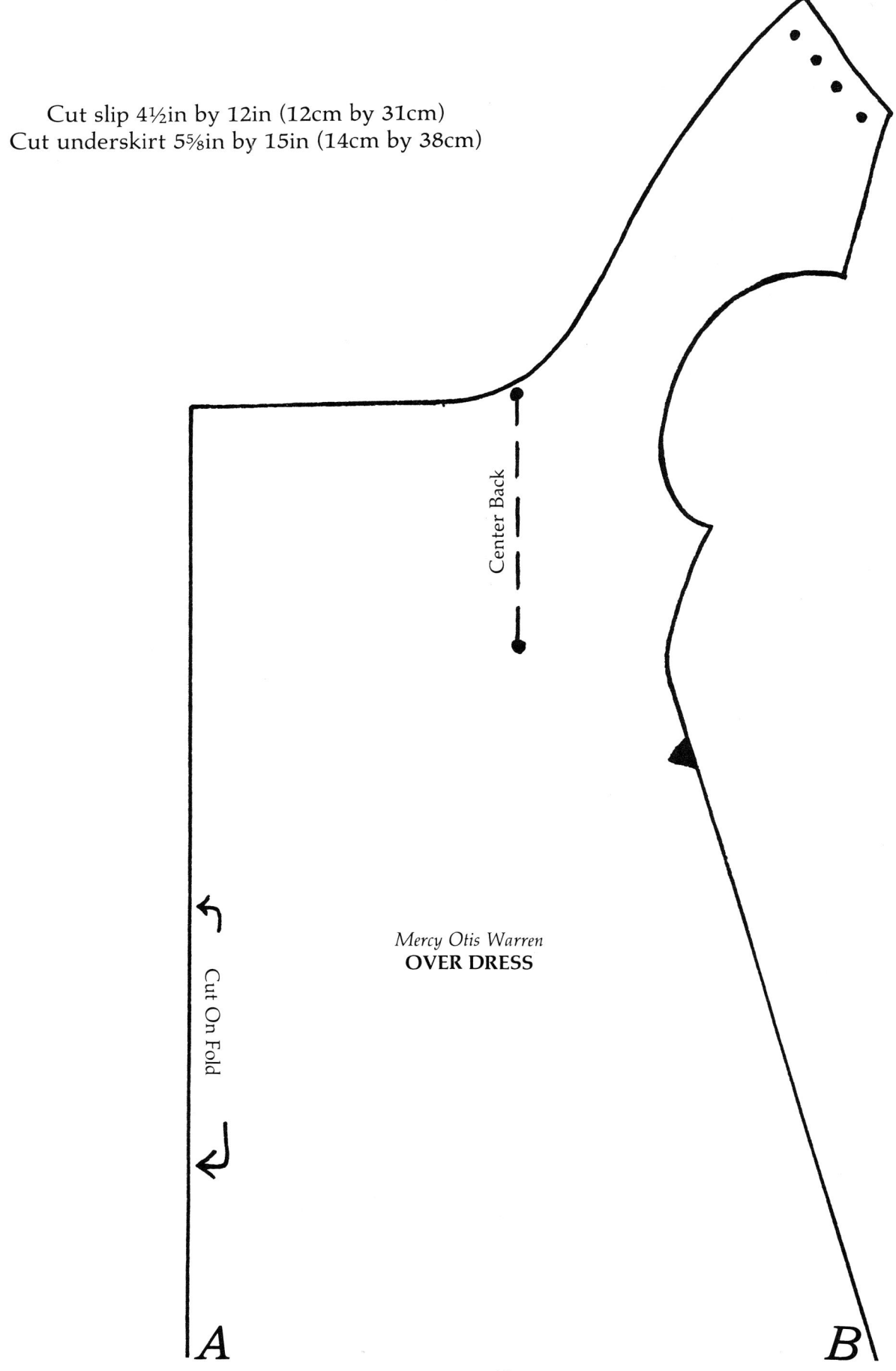

A B

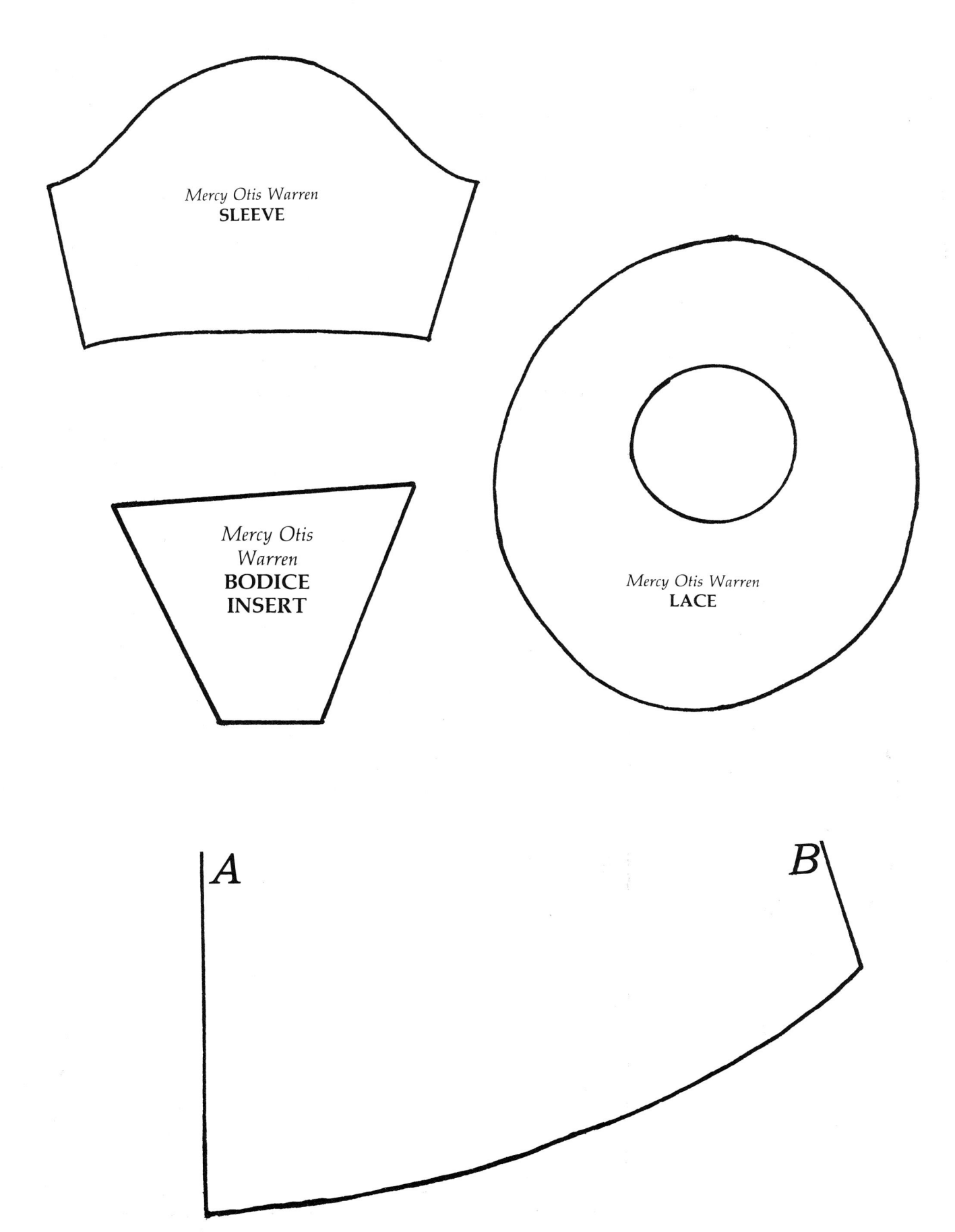

Mercy Otis Warren
SLEEVE

Mercy Otis Warren
BODICE INSERT

Mercy Otis Warren
LACE

A

B

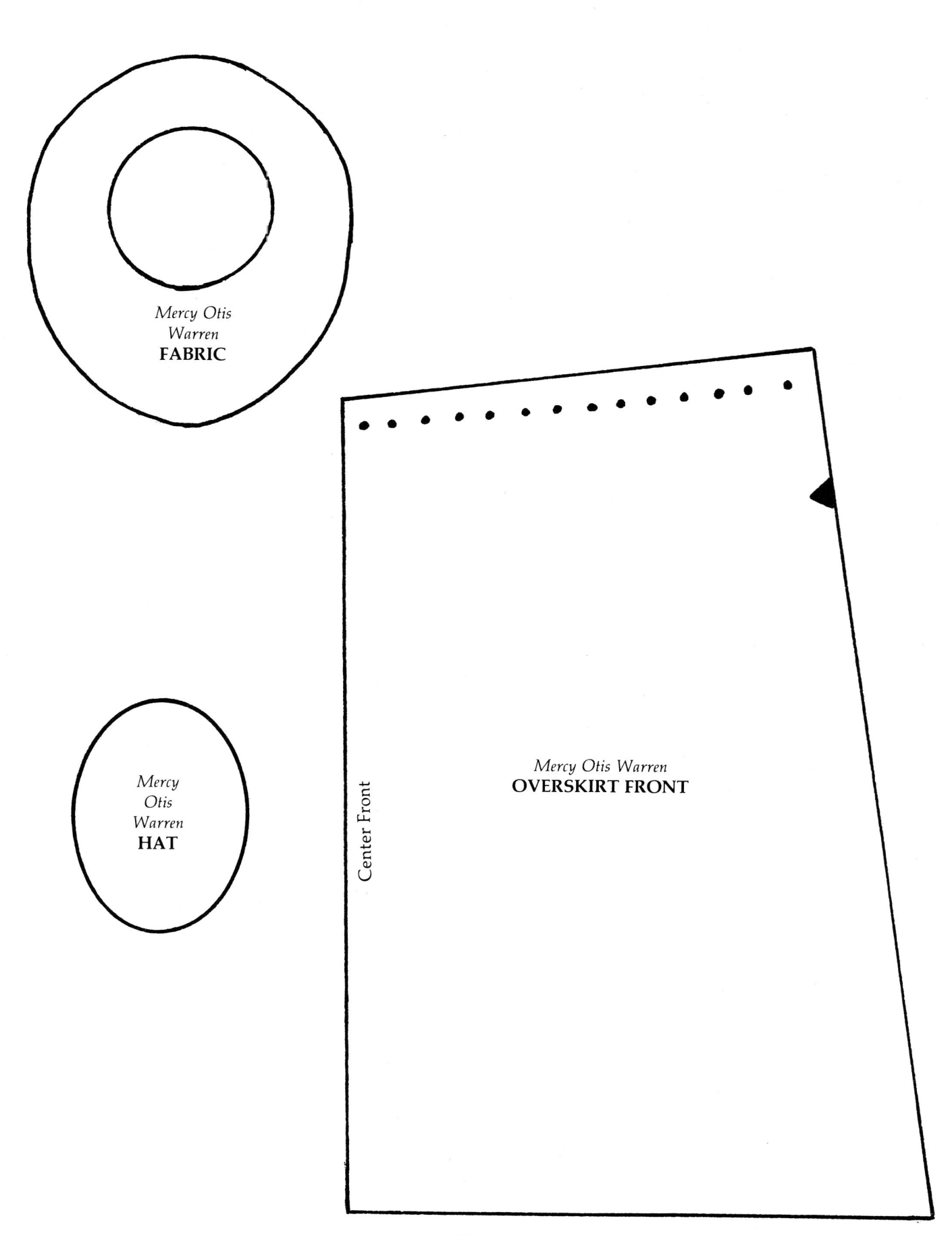

Mercy Otis Warren
FABRIC

Mercy Otis Warren
HAT

Mercy Otis Warren
OVERSKIRT FRONT

Center Front

Margaret Sanger

Margaret Sanger
BODICE
Cut skirt 4⅞in (12.5cm) by 13½in (34cm)

Center Back

Fold

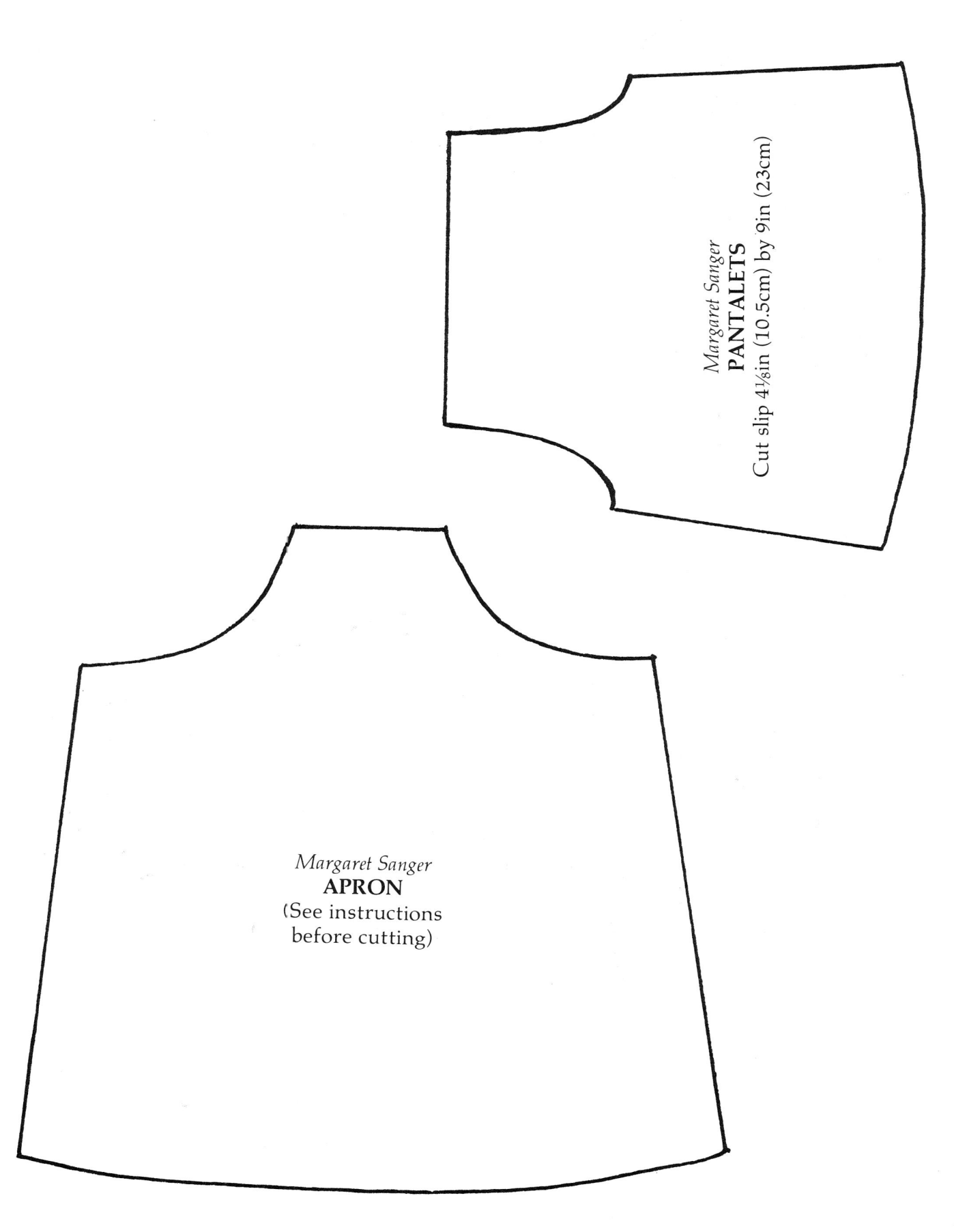

Margaret Sanger
PANTALETS
Cut slip 4⅛in (10.5cm) by 9in (23cm)

Margaret Sanger
APRON
(See instructions before cutting)

Harriet Tubman

Harriet Tubman
LOWER BACK BODICE

Fold

Harriet Tubman
SKIRT A

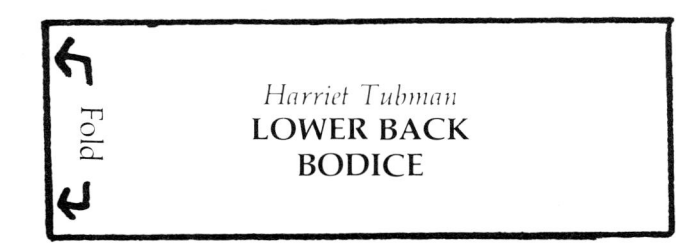

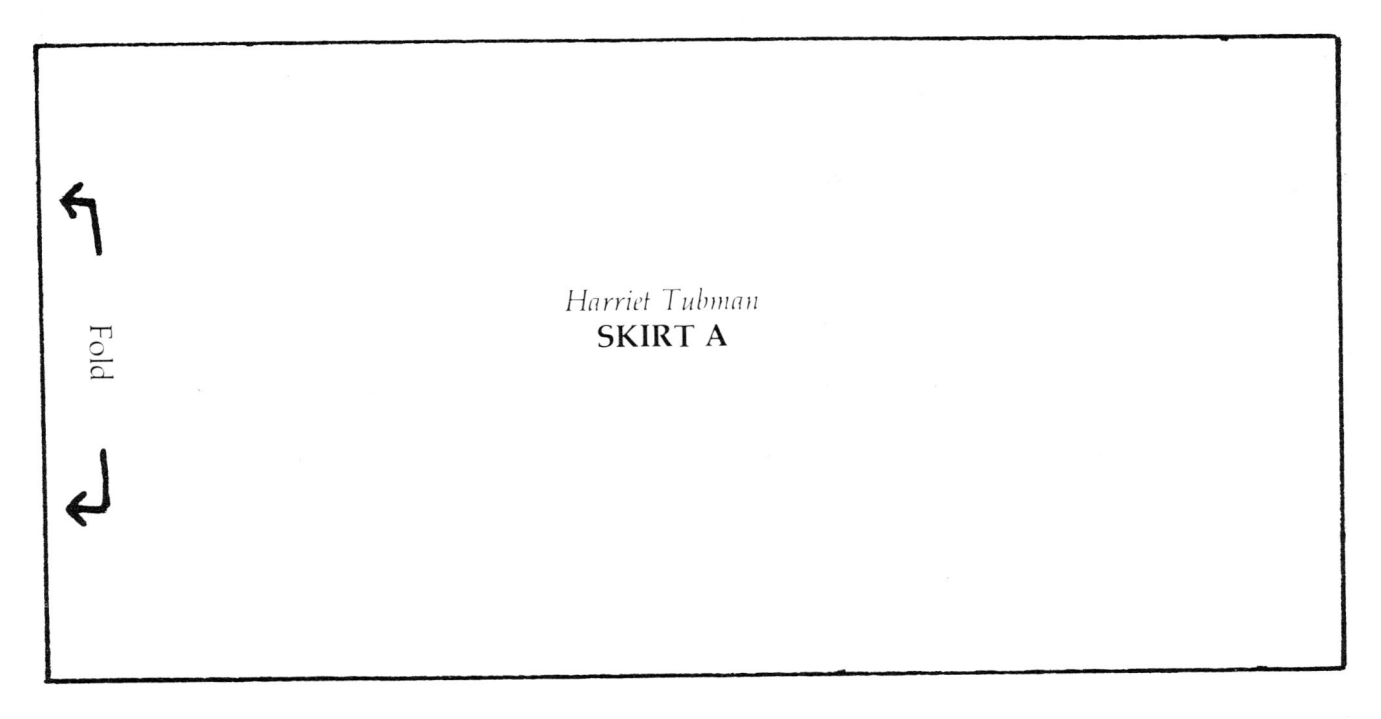

Fold

See Margaret Sanger pattern for underwear instructions.

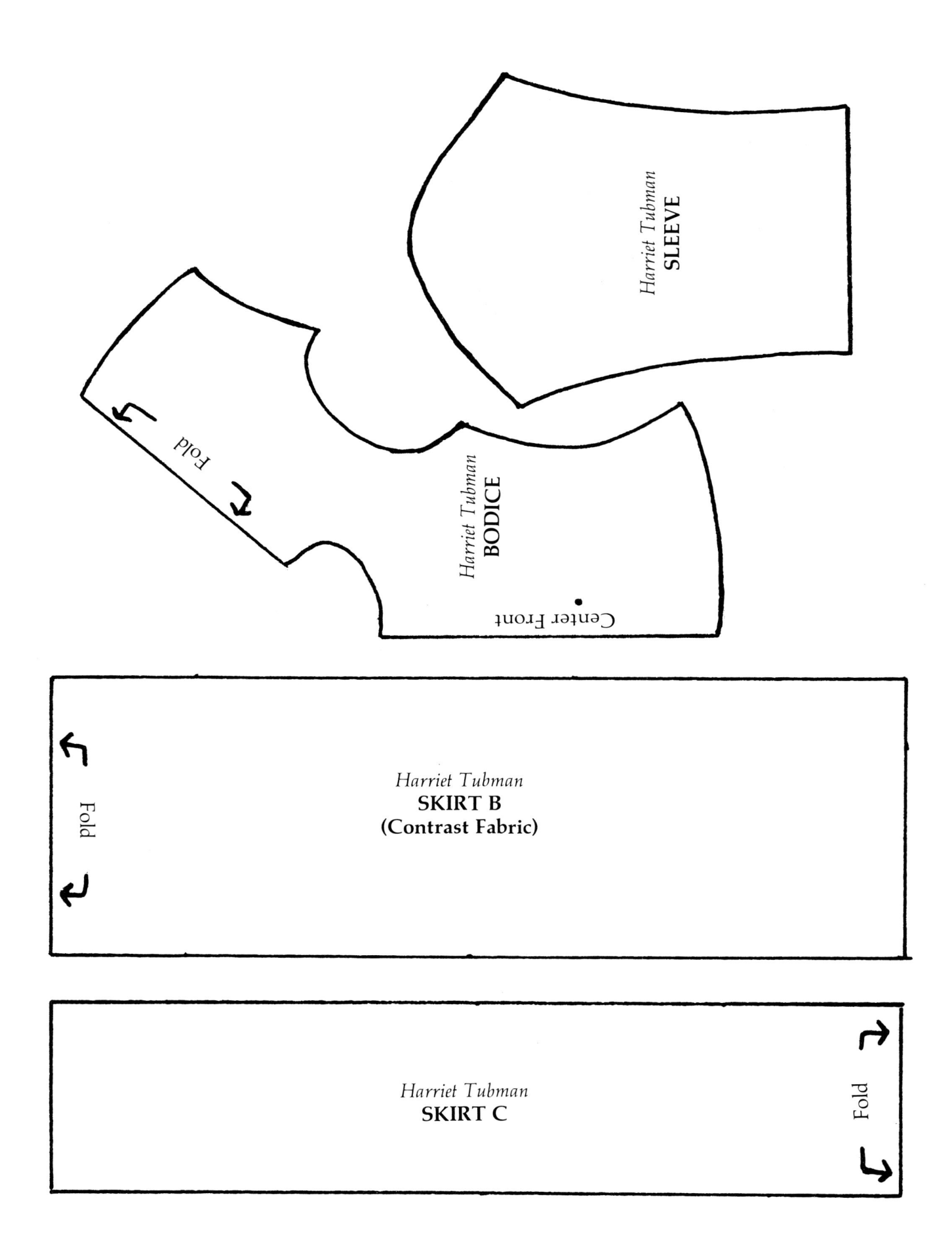

Harriet Tubman
SLEEVE

Harriet Tubman
BODICE

Center Front

Fold

Harriet Tubman
SKIRT B
(Contrast Fabric)

Fold

Harriet Tubman
SKIRT C

Fold

Bibliography

Backus, Jean L. *Letters from Amelia.* Beacon Press, 1982.

Encyclopedia Americana, The. Danbury, Connecticut: Grolier Inc.

Engle, Paul. *Women in the American Revolution.* Chicago: Follett Publishing Co., 1976.

Franklin, John Hope. *Black Americans.* New York: Time-Life Books, 1970.

Gray, Madeline. *Margaret Sanger.* New York: Richard March Publishers, 1979.

Kaller, Otto. *Grandma Moses.* New York: Harry N. Abrams, Inc., 1975.

Sweet, Frederick A. *Miss Mary Cassatt.* University of Oklahoma Press, 1966.

BOOKS BY THE AUTHOR

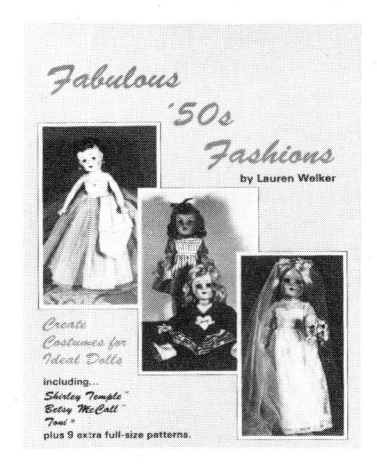

Fabulous '50s Fashions
by Lauren Welker
Beautiful 1950s doll outfits can easily be made from the patterns and instructions (Miss Revlon, Betsy Wetsy, Toni, Betsy McCall & others). 60 pages, 8¼ x 10⅞in. Paperback.
ISBN: 0-87588-223-4
Item #2867 **$4.95**
(plus $1.25 postage)

Fashions to Fit Ginny & Jill
by Lauren Welker
Six 1950s pattern outfits for each doll: 10½in Jill and 8in Ginny. These outfits will fit many other dolls from the time period. 32 pages, 8¼ x 10⅞in. Paperback.
ISBN: 0-87588-183-1
Item #912 **$4.95**
(plus $1.25 postage)

Six Famous American Women
A Doll Maker's Workbook
by Lauren Welker
Designed to teach the basics of making a quality original doll. Two body patterns are included - one for use with full length arms and legs and one for use with half arms and legs. Patterns for 5½in (14cm) tall or 8in (20cm) doll of Grandma Moses, Amelia Earhart, Mary Cassatt, Mercy Otis Warren, Margaret Sanger and Harriet Tubman. Detailed instructions for modeling each of the dolls from a polyform clay, baking and painting plus making felt bodies. Paperback.
ISBN: 0-87588-290-0
Item #3448 **$5.95**
(plus $1.25 postage)

Available at distinctive doll dealers, toy stores and book stores, or directly from the publisher, Hobby House Press, Inc., 900 Frederick St., Cumberland, MD 21502.